The Shoes that
Love Made

The Shoes that Love Made

Paul Brand

Lucille Travis

CF4·K

For Joshua:
May your heart know the shoes Love has made
for your feet, and may his love guide you all the days
of your life.

10 9 8 7 6 5 4 3 2 1
© Copyright 2011 Lucille Travis
ISBN: 978-1-84550-630-8

Published by
Christian Focus Publications
Geanies House, Fearn, Ross-shire,
IV20 1TW, Scotland, UK.
www.christianfocus.com
email: info@christianfocus.com

Cover design by Daniel van Straaten
Illustrated by Brent Donoho
Printed and bound in Denmark by Nørhaven Paperback

Contents

On the Mountains of Death

Darkness blanketed the thick forests on the Kolli Malai mountain range of southern India. In the remote mission settlement high on a mountain a single lamp shone from inside the mission house. Paul and his young sister, Connie, had already been sent to their beds. Paul could hear Connie's soft breathing as she slept. From under the tent of mosquito netting over his bed he lay listening to the night sounds. Only a week ago a large cheetah had stolen one of the goats from the mission corral. Paul pictured his father camped out in one of the isolated mountain villages, listening to some of the same sounds. His father had been gone now for four days, tending the sick, teaching about Jesus, and helping the villagers. Paul wished he was there camping out by his father's side with Connie and his mother the way they often did when he took them along to help, but this time he had ridden off on his horse by himself. Paul and his sister and mother were alone in the mission compound. Besides his family, there were no other white-skinned people in any of these mountains.

The scratching of his mother's pen on paper caught his attention. Paul's father had built their house like a long train and from each room one could look into the next. From the bedroom Paul could see to the kitchen where his mother sat at the table writing letters. The letters she wrote would be mailed back to a place called England where his parents had lived before they became missionaries to India. Many were letters to family that neither Paul nor Connie had ever seen. They had never seen England either. Paul didn't mind. He loved the mountains, had plenty of friends, all of them dark-skinned, and this was his home here in India.

A sudden knock at the door brought Paul sitting straight up. A man stood in the doorway, the light of the torch in his hand showed his dark-skinned face. Paul listened as his mother and the villager spoke in Tamil, the language of the people of the Kolli Hills. Paul knew Tamil well. His mother quickly began to pack her medical bag.

"Someone in his village needs help," she said as Paul came to stand beside her. "I need to go, but God will take care of you, and you must help him by taking care of your sister, Connie." In a moment his mother was gone, disappearing down the twisting mountain path until Paul could no longer see the light of the torch held by the villager or his mother's lantern. His five-year-old heart beat fast as he watched the darkness fill the path where his mother and her guide had been. Paul glanced at his three-year-old sister, Connie, sleeping soundly under the heavy mosquito netting over her bed.

The buzz of a mosquito sent Paul running to the shelter of his own bed and its protective netting. Here in the Kolli Malai or Mountains of Death, the people's name for this mountain range, all had reason to fear the dreaded mosquitoes. By sunset swarms of mosquitoes that carried malaria appeared. There were other terrible diseases here too like blackwater fever and dysentery that attacked both the Tamil people of the hills and those who chose to come there. Few chose to come that did not live there.

As he lay huddled on his bed Paul thought he heard animal footsteps outside, perhaps a cheetah? Fear sent a shiver through him. He knew his mother had gone because nothing was more important than helping the people come to know Jesus. That meant taking care of the sick, the wounded, and even pulling rotted teeth, a continual need among the people. His parents did all those things. Paul glanced at the sleeping Connie. The two of them had already agreed that when they were older that was what they would do too, teach about Jesus. He could hear mosquitoes whining about his bed making him glad he was under the thick netting. His eyelids felt heavy but he mustn't sleep. He needed to stay awake and watch for Connie and himself. Propped against his pillow he wondered which animals might come too close to the house on their hunt for food. Weary but awake he listened hard for signals of any danger near. It felt to him that hours had dragged by, broken only by sudden noises that brought him wide awake to listen until they faded away. Paul knew he would not forget this night, alone waiting and wondering, listening, afraid to close his eyes and fall asleep.

A hard rain began to fall, slapping against the tin roof of the house and splatting on the stone veranda. Before long it drummed against everything, shutting out all the other noises. Paul yawned mightily. The next thing he knew the sun was shining and his mother was home singing a song as she prepared breakfast. Young as he was then, Paul was right; he would always remember his night alone on the Kollis with his little sister.

There were many things he needed to remember, like the tiny scorpions that lived under the bark of certain trees or the larger ones that roamed at night near the outhouse. Neither Paul nor Connie or any of their Tamil friends wore shoes. Paul's foot had been stung once by a small scorpion, a painful memory. Now he watched carefully which trees he climbed and where he stepped at night. Snakes were another thing to remember and his father had taught him to respect and avoid those like the cobras, vipers, and deadly adders. One snake, the eleven step cobra, his father said was called that because once a man was bitten by it he would get no farther than eleven steps before falling dead. Like his Tamil Indian friends, Paul did not let fears keep him from climbing the highest trees, swinging from the vines, exploring the forests, and sometimes taking wild rides through the rice fields on the water buffalo. Connie, who was his constant shadow, had soon learned to do whatever things her small chubby legs could handle and was just as fearless.

The morning mountain air felt clear and cool, and Paul longed to be off running with his friends, but his mother was already preparing his schoolwork. With a basket, a rope, and his lesson book she marched Paul outside. Together they walked to the tall tree Paul called his school. Handing him one end of the rope to tie around his waist, she attached the basket holding his school supplies to the other end. "Up you go," she said. "When you think you have them done correctly, let down the basket and I will check them. If you are right you may come down, but if not I will send them back up to you to do again." When Paul couldn't concentrate on his lessons seated at the kitchen table, his mother had come up with the idea of doing them in his favorite place: high in a tree. It proved to be a grand solution, and Paul minded less doing his schoolwork perched in his tree.

The lessons he did enjoy, and Connie too, were the ones that came from his beloved father who studied nature and loved sharing his findings with his children. Every camping trip, each hike into the forest brought new things to explore. His tall, cheerful father always had some new thing to tell them about. One time his father opened a giant ant mound to show them the insides of the nests. Paul learned about army ants, cricket hunters, curious plant traps, and the endless wonders of India's forests and animals. His father's keen observations and curiosity made him Paul's favorite teacher. Today his father was headed to a remote mountain village and taking Paul and Connie along to help with the work.

Connie had stopped to pick up a fallen breadfruit. Her hands were sticky with its sap-like juice. "Oh, oh," she said, and threw it from her. As she wiped her hands on a patch of grass, Paul shook his head. Both of them would need to scrub their hands once their father started treating wounds. It would be their job to hand him bandages and ointment, and whatever else he needed.

"You suppose Papa will have to use his knife today?" Connie asked in a small voice. She hated the sight of the knife and would turn her face away each time their father had to use it on a patient.

"Girls are sissies," Paul said. "You don't see me turning my eyes away." He didn't add that he too wished he never had to watch his father operate on a wound again. But it was not to be.

In the distance ahead of them were the clusters of round thatched-roof houses and the fields of green rice paddies that stretched behind the village. They were still a ways from the village when an older man leaning heavily on the shoulder of a young man came limping towards them. Paul stared at the man's hugely swollen leg. The man groaned with each step he took.

Paul's father hurried to meet them, his medical bag already in his hands. He was kneeling and examining the leg when Connie and Paul reached them.

His father spoke in Tamil to the men, and pointed to a grassy spot off the trail. Turning to Paul and Connie he said, "I'll need you to hold the bandages and ointment, children. We'll set up supplies under that tree over there, Paul, and you can bring the bag with the bandages." Paul nodded.

Connie stood still biting her lip as Paul arranged their traveling packs and selected the one with the rolls of bandages. He placed one hand on her shoulder. "Come on. Let's just get this over," he said. In the few moments ahead as his father operated on the man's leg, Paul felt himself gag and wanted to turn away. The leg was badly infected. As he watched, sickened by the sight and wishing for it to be over quickly, he wondered how his father could operate in spite of the patient's terrible moans.

His father had nothing to keep a patient from feeling the pain as he operated. Usually the patient would cling hard to a relative or friend until it was over. This time the man had cried out as the knife came down into the swollen leg releasing a torrent of pus and blood such as Paul had never seen before. The smell of infection was overpowering. When it was finally over and Paul could turn away he knew for certain that he would never ever become a doctor. He hated the things that went with it: sewing up wounds, cutting out infections, the blood, the disgusting sight and smell of infection, the suffering.

They had not been back at the mission long before Paul was certain he had made the right decision never to become a doctor. It wasn't just how disgusting and awful it could be; treating some diseases could be dangerous.

Paul and Connie had both finished their schoolwork for the day and were heading towards the forest of trees nearby when their mother's voice brought them to a standstill. "Paul, Connie, go into the house immediately and stay there until I come for you." As usual Connie, who could be counted on to obey, turned back to the house. Paul followed slowly, ready to question his mother until he saw what his mother had already seen: three strangers, their feet wrapped in bloody rags, coming up the trail to the mission. The men lifted their hands in the Indian greeting palms together, and Paul gasped. Where some fingers should have been were small stubs or none at all and the others were bent into claw-like shapes. Whatever was the matter with these men it was so bad that Paul's mother would not allow them to even stay and watch their father work on them as they usually did. Quickly Paul hid behind the corner of the house where he could still see and not be seen.

Paul's father hurried toward the men greeting them in Tamil. His father had brought a bucket of water to cleanse their feet and fresh bandages, but as he worked Paul saw that he wore gloves. Paul shifted his weight quietly. His father was kneeling near the men as Paul had so often seen him do with his patients. Only this time his father did not probe their wounds. As he unwrapped their bloody bandages, Paul saw the missing toes, the stubs of feet, and the terrible infected ulcers. His father's gloved hands did not actually touch their feet without the thick pad of bandages he held. He seemed to be wasting bandages, layering them thickly between himself and the men's skin. When he was finished he did not pick up the soiled pads but left them lying in a heap on the ground where he had dropped them. Finally, his father stood and let the gloves slip from his hands onto the pile, spoke something softly and turned away towards the washing shed holding his hands before him.

Now would be the time Paul knew his mother would offer the men food before they left for their village. This time she came from the house holding a basket of fruit and bread and set it down a few feet away from the men. "You may keep the basket," she called to them. Curious, Paul wondered why his mother would give them one of her few baskets and why she did not sit with them as she usually did with those who came for help.

Still in his hiding place, Paul watched as the men ate. His father too stood nearby watching. Why wasn't he sitting with the men and talking to them, Paul wondered. When the patients had eaten, they stood, thanked his father in the Tamil way and left. They did not take the basket.

Paul couldn't wait any longer. "Father," he called as he came towards the spot where the men had been sitting, "who were those men?"

"Stop right where you are, Paul," his father commanded sternly. "Neither you or Connie are to play anywhere near that spot. You are not to walk or sit where those men sat. You must obey me in this, son." As he spoke his father set the small pile of soiled bandages on fire and then the empty basket. "The men are lepers, son, and anything they touched must be burned. Leprosy is a terrible disease, dangerous to anyone who comes in contact with it. Do you understand, Paul?"

"Yes," Paul replied. "I promise not to go anywhere near that place, and I'll see to it that Connie doesn't either." Paul thought of the Bible stories about lepers. How awful leprosy was and it was a dangerous and ugly disease. Paul wanted nothing to do with it.

With a shiver Paul turned back to the house to fetch Connie. He would gladly be a missionary, but not a doctor, not ever. There were plenty of other things to do. He would not mind so much pulling teeth for the villagers. Tooth pain was terrible and people came wanting their teeth pulled. Often the crowds applauded when the tooth came out because they knew the pain would stop. Even his mother, small as she was, would help pull the villagers' aching teeth. Usually the patient would help her by pulling away from her as she gripped her forceps around the bad tooth. Her motto was "place the forceps down as far as you can around the bad tooth and don't let go." Paul would gladly give out medicines and bandages, but someone else could do the operating and care for the lepers. He could even be a builder like his father who had built their house and all the buildings they had needed.

Connie met him at the door. "Are they gone yet?" she asked looking up at Paul. He knew she wanted him to explain everything that had happened. He did, and sitting at the kitchen table Paul went on to assure her that when they were old enough to be missionaries there were lots of things they would do. They could teach the people still unreached in the mountains around them how to farm better and keep their wells clean, lots of good things. "The most important thing we need to do," Paul said, "is to tell them about Jesus." Paul stood up and beckoned Connie to the window. "Look out there," he said pointing to the mountain peaks rising around their own mountain top. "All those mountains" he said, "have hidden villages where no missionary has gone yet. That's where we'll go." Connie nodded her agreement. She was content with their plans. Paul drew in a deep breath of mountain air. He and Connie had never dreamed of living anywhere else but here in India, or of being anything else but missionaries. He just wouldn't be a doctor.

In England you wear Shoes

For weeks Paul and Connie had seen little of their parents. It was the year 1918, the year that an epidemic of Spanish influenza had broken out and spread throughout the world. It reached even the remote villages of the Kolli Hills and many were dying. Fear of catching the disease made whole families of villagers flee into the forests leaving all who were sick to care for themselves. The pujari, priest of the village, refused to leave his house to help anyone. The sick desperately needed nourishment but were too ill to care for themselves. Paul's father and mother went from outpost to outpost tending the sick villagers day and night. In the mission kitchen steam filled the air above the giant black pot of boiling rice-water, kept boiling night and day as pot after pot of the thin soup was made to spoon feed to patients who would otherwise die from dehydration. It seemed that each week brought news of new cases, as well as those who had died of the disease. At last there were almost no new cases. This morning their own father, worn out with the work and sick with a fever, had stayed in bed. Paul and Connie quietly slipped outdoors to let him rest.

Connie tugged at Paul's shirt. "Does father have the influenza?" she asked in a loud whisper.

"No, nothing like it," Paul replied, his gaze bent on a large insect crawling close to his foot.

"What does it look like?" Connie demanded.

In his most confident five-year-old manner, Paul explained. "You can't see it, but it makes you cough, and feel sick, so you can't eat or drink and you dry up with fever, and look awful." Paul had heard all this from his young friend, Nambi, whose grandfather was one of those nursed by Paul's father.

Connie pulled on Paul's shirt again. Her eyes were wide. "Paulie, that's how you looked when you put your neck in the banyan vine and hung yourself."

Paul remembered that incident all too well. They had been camping on one of his father's preaching tours when it happened. Paul and some of the village boys were swinging from vines in the banyan trees. Someone had tied two of the vines to form a loop, and Paul swinging on his vine did not see the loop until it suddenly caught about his neck jerking tight and suspending him in midair. "I didn't put my neck in that vine," he said. "It just slipped over my head and choked me while I was swinging. And I didn't really get hung, just almost. Mother came running when you screamed for her and she said I was only out for awhile after she got me down. When I woke up in bed my neck was pretty sore, but that's not influenza."

"I'm glad you didn't get hanged really good," Connie said looking up at Paul, her blue eyes already gathering tears. Before Paul could say more, a shout from the path that led up to the mission house made them both look.

Two of the villagers were coming swiftly along the path, one of them calling out. "Hurry, call your father, the pujari and his wife are sick." Paul's mother hurried from the house and was soon on her way following the two men down the path, her medical bag in hand. The pujari in the nearby village was the local priest and leader of the worship of spirits. He secretly opposed the preaching about Jesus to his people, threatening the wrath of the gods to anyone who became a Christian. Some of the mission's cows were poisoned, and Paul's family knew his threats could mean physical harm to them as well. Paul hid whenever he saw the priest. So far none of the villagers had dared to disobey the pujari, and though they welcomed all the help the missionaries brought, almost no one attended the little chapel Paul's father had built and preached in each Sunday. Now Paul's parents were the only ones who dared to help the sick priest and his family. His mother had gone gladly to see what needed to be done.

For the rest of the morning Paul and Connie took turns peeking in at their father to be sure he was only sleeping. By noon Paul's mother returned with the sad news that the pujari and his wife were both dying and leaving behind a young boy and a tiny frail baby girl. It was the custom of the Tamil people to leave orphans and unwanted babies by the roadside to die. The pujari wanted Paul's father to come and take his tiny baby girl to the mission house. Unless the missionaries took the baby and cared for it, the villagers would let the pujari's child die. At last the pujari had seen the difference between the demon gods of his people and this Swami who taught of a Jesus who cared for the sick and dying, and he wanted both his children to learn about Jesus. Paul's father was the only one the pujari trusted to care for the baby and her older brother. Paul's father rose from his sick bed and left quickly for the pujari's house.

Paul watched his father leave, and a few days later after the death of the pujari and his wife, the tiny baby girl came to live at the mission house and her older brother to stay at the boarding school. The baby, soon named Ruth, was so small and sick, no one knew if she would live. To the astonishment of the villagers Paul's mother cared for the little one constantly and the baby survived! Paul and Connie were both delighted with the new addition to the family. Her brother, Aaron, visited his sister and her caregivers whenever he wished. There was no legal adoption, and in the Tamil way a few years later both Ruth and Aaron would stay in India when Paul and his family went to England on furlough. While he and Connie were away at school in England, little Ruth would live with his parents and Aaron attend the mission school. To Paul and Connie they would always be their adopted Tamil sister and brother. Years later when Paul's mother returned alone to continue her work in the Kollis Ruth helped with the mission work until she left to marry a Christian teacher.

No villager had dared to become a Christian in the six years Paul's father had preached in the Kollis, but now with the pujari gone the church began to see newcomers. The example before them of love and caring the people saw in little Ruth's rescue and her brother Aaron was a new thing and now they felt free to come and learn of the Jesus who taught such things. Some gave their hearts to him, and the mission work grew, spreading to the outposts where new schools and clinics were built and the good news about Jesus taught.

Paul and Connie grew too. Though he and Connie still helped his father on their camping visits to villages, now that Paul was older he had other duties like helping his father each Sunday morning make ready the mud-walled chapel his father had built for morning services.

This Sunday morning an hour before church began they walked together to the small thatched roof chapel. It was Paul's special job to set up the long mats before the people arrived. There were no windows to shut out the morning sounds of the forest as he worked, nothing between his feet and the hard-packed earth floor as he carefully pulled the mats into place. This was the church Paul had grown up in for all of his eight-and-a-half-years, the one his father preached in, the one where he and Connie sang loudly along with the dark-skinned friends who came. The last mat slid into place but Paul didn't move. His mind was far away.

What would it be like when they left the Kollis? Last night his father had explained that they were going back to the land far across the sea where they had come from before Paul had been born. They were leaving for a year on what was known as a furlough, a time to visit family and churches in England. Standing in the little chapel Paul continued to daydream until he felt a large hand on his shoulder and looked up to see his tall father's smiling face.

"What are you thinking about, son?" he asked.

"If we are gone, father," Paul said, "who will take over my job of setting the mats in place?"

His father patted his shoulder. "Don't worry, Paul. We will see that someone takes on that job before we leave." Satisfied, Paul nodded his head, but within minutes he was once again daydreaming.

What would the church in far away England be like? Though he had seen the sea in pictures, he had no idea what the real sea would look like, or the place called England, and they were leaving in a few weeks. Paul loved the idea of an adventure, but leaving home, the Kollis, and all their friends to go to a place where he didn't know anyone, seemed like too big a price to pay for an adventure. He was glad it would only be for a time, a furlough, and then they would return home to India.

Word of their leaving spread quickly. The following week, high in a breadfruit tree as Paul leaned against its trunk and placed a bare foot on the limb below him his friend, Nambi, on the limb above him called down, "Is it true you are leaving the Kollis to go over the big water to see your white family?" Intent on keeping his balance Paul began to climb down before he answered. Below them Nurugan and Senthil, boys from the nearby village waited, their dark skin shining against their white loincloths. Standing by them, Connie rubbed one sticky leg against the other spreading the thick breadfruit sap over most of her.

"It's true," Paul answered in Tamil. "But it's just for a visit. We'll be back." He slid down the rest of the tree and landed softly. "We don't leave for three weeks yet." As Paul stood up a shiver came over him, then another. Quickly he glanced at the sky. It was late afternoon and just about the time that it always happened. "Snakes time" he said loudly and began to run back to the mission house. Behind him Nambi and the others watched, understanding well what he meant. "Snakes time" was their code name for an attack of malaria. The sickness made the body writhe in chills and fever like a snake's writhing movements. All of them knew from their own experience that a dreaded attack of malaria had come upon Paul. The attacks came suddenly and because there was no cure for malaria one could count on its return. No one knew just when it might fall, though it was often at this time of day that one began. Connie began running after Paul and calling for their mother. She too knew the meaning.

Paul went straight to his bed and pulled the wool blanket up to his neck. A freezing coldness gripped him so that his whole body shook, writhing like a snake's. He would soon be burning up with fever. Minutes later his mother came bringing the quinine that would help him. A frantic Connie followed her. She was not yet sick but would probably soon be. There was little else to do but wait for the quinine to work and until then huddle down under the blankets.

The quinine did its work but now Paul had little time to roam the forest with his friends. For ten years his father and mother had not left the Kollis. Where there had been no schools, no teacher, no doctor, there was now a small boarding school at the mission compound, and five other small schools his father had built in the remote villages. The work of the mission would go on with the help of a teacher and a doctor until they returned. Paul and Connie helped on visits to each of the villages where his father preached, and all of them said their goodbyes. At last they were ready and the final day had come.

The descent from the Kollis had not changed since Paul's father first brought Paul's mother to the top as a new bride. The monsoon rains had come on that day, and Paul liked to hear the story of his young mother arriving on the mountain in her drenched and muddy wedding dress. At least this time the rains did not come. The only way down was steep. From 4,000 feet above the valley the narrow path twisted and turned in hairpin turns sharply over rough rocky ground and through leech-filled, weedy brush. Connie and his mother rode in a dholi, a canvas hammock lashed to bamboo poles and carried by strong Tamil men. Paul, with his feet bare as usual, carried his backpack and followed behind his father. Several times he stopped to pick the thin black leeches from his legs. His mother had agreed to take the shoes Paul would need later in the litter with her. Who needed shoes? Not Paul, and not any of his Tamil friends, not even Connie needed them.

They were down at last and Paul turned to look back at the mountains rising sharply to tower above the plains, their thick forests and clouded slopes a grand sight.

They would be gone for a whole year, and Paul already longed to be back home.

At his mother's call he hurried to catch up. For the next five miles of the trip they would ride in a jutka, a reed-topped wagon pulled by a pony. Soon enough all thoughts of the mission on the Kollis gave way to the wonders of the Indian countryside.

As the train flew across the land, flashing by women in saris carrying great baskets of dung on their heads, men in white loincloths, long-horned cattle, and children playing, Paul watched fascinated. The land seemed to go on and on, full of colors and brilliant sun. "Smell that?" Paul asked Connie who looked up sleepily. "That's the smell of jasmine," he said proudly. Flowers and herbs with sweet heavy smells were as much a part of India as the heat and the monsoon rains.

When they arrived at the sea Paul stared unbelieving at the ships and the crowded docks, and the great sea before them. But nothing could have prepared him or Connie for the morning of their landing in Tilbury, England. A crowd of white people waited to welcome them, all of them strangers, and all of them somehow related to his family.

The hugging and joyful welcoming descended on Paul and Connie as well as his mother and father. When at last his family was once more on its way, this time to the house where they would be living, Paul discovered that his feet hurt. Shoes that he didn't mind once or twice a year on a visit to the mission station in Madras, India, were now supposed to stay on his feet, all day. He reached down to run a finger around the edges of his shoe. Nothing helped but a questioning look at his mother received a firm shake of the head and Paul knew he was not to take them off. He could hardly wait until they got to the aunts' house where his father said they would stay. He'd take them off as soon as they were there and not put them on again. He could always just carry them.

Left Behind

"This is it, Paul, we are in St. John's Wood and this is your aunts' house where we will be staying," his father said. Paul stood and stared at the narrow, gray-brick four-story house set between two stone walls. "Your aunts call it Nethania," his father said and smiled. "It means gift of God, and Aunt Hope and Aunt Eunice have lived here for thirty years."

"Do they live here all alone?" Connie asked tugging at her mother's skirt.

"Yes, along with Grandmother and the help, dear" Paul's mother answered. "The aunts have always lived together, kept the house, and cared for Grandmother ever since your grandfather passed away. You will find them very proper English women, but as kind and good as can be. Come now, we mustn't keep them waiting."

Paul followed last as they were ushered inside the hallway. What he saw before him sent a shiver of excitement running through him. The two thin straight ladies that were the aunts looked outwardly as stately as the house but their faces were full of joy as they welcomed Paul's family with warm words and hugs. And just behind them was the most magnificent

curved stairway Paul had ever seen! Inching towards it
he stared upwards and saw that it must go all the way
to the top, right to the fourth floor! Now it was his
turn to be hugged and exclaimed over, but in the back
of his mind Paul had plans for that stairway.

Once they were settled in and Paul's parents had
left on a trip to visit with the mission board members
and supporters of their work, Paul went into action.
The aunts were taking afternoon rests. Grandmother,
who was an invalid and never left her room on the
third floor, was surely asleep too. Paul and Connie
were on their own at last. "Look how easy it is," Paul
explained to Connie as he straddled the stair banister
on the third floor. "Just hold on tight and away we
go." Connie laughed and did exactly as she always
did: follow Paul's example. They flew down the long,
twisting banister and landed with a thud on the thick
carpeting bare inches away from a white statue on a
pedestal. It was only the beginning of what would turn
out to be great fun for the two of them, but terror
for the aunts and the help. Grandmother, with whom
the children visited quietly each evening in her room
on the third floor, never knew of Paul and Connie's
daring feats, their fearless attempts to climb and run
as they had in the Kolli Hills of India.

The aunts' house seemed much like a museum.
Windows were tall with heavy drapes in rooms
filled with displays of precious statues, paintings, and
collections of expensive pottery. Paul felt a desperate

need to climb but there were no trees available. Inside the house Paul soon had the idea of using the great parlor to practice climbing. He invented a way for Connie and himself to go from one side of the parlor to the other without putting their feet on the floor. He had just completed a climb from one high cabinet to the top of a nearby bookcase when the parlor door swung open. "No, no, children, you simply cannot climb on the parlor furniture or the window frames," Aunt Eunice pleaded. Paul froze in place. The older of his two aunts stood in the doorway with her hand over her heart. "Your grandfather's fine collection of pottery is displayed here, and you will surely be crashing into it," she said. Paul didn't argue. The house was full of statues and pottery and things on pedestals, but he knew how to avoid them all. He and Connie made it a practice whenever they were alone, not to walk but to climb around the rooms from one piece of furniture to the next even swinging across on the heavy drapes, and they were quite good at it!

Aunt Hope had come to the parlor to help her sister. Although as proper in manners as her sister, she allowed herself the one exception of running up or down the stairs instead of walking, and whistling. But not even Aunt Hope could allow for Paul and Connie's wild ways. "Now, children, why don't you run along and play outside until dinner time?" she suggested.

When the door closed behind Connie and Paul, their Aunt Eunice sighed deeply and collapsed into a chair. Aunt Hope smiled, and patted her shoulder. "Remember, dear, those children haven't even seen a house like this before, nor any of the things we take for granted, not even a bathtub. They will learn proper ways in time." She sighed and suddenly brought a hand to her mouth. "Oh, my, I hope they remembered this time to put on their shoes before they went outside."

Not only were Paul's feet bare but Connie's too. There weren't any tall trees to climb near the aunts' house, but the tall lampposts with their cross bars just below the lanterns were a fair substitute. Astonished passers-by stared up at something they had never seen before: two young children hanging from the tops of the lamppost cross bars by the backs of their knees! For Paul, as for Connie, hanging like a monkey was an easy skill learned years ago in the Kolli Hills. Together they were about to drive both the help and their aunts to distraction when their freedom finally came to a halt.

Both were enrolled in school. Back in the Kollis Paul might have done all his lessons seated high in a tree near the mission house. Now he looked at the walls of his new schoolroom, smooth, white walls enclosing a room full of desks where others like himself sat waiting for the headmistress to speak. His new headmistress looked up at the class with eyes that seemed to say "No nonsense tolerated here," and Paul soon found that she was strict and demanding. Paul had much to learn, not the least of which was how to keep his shoes on all day in spite of his longing to kick them off. With the help of an older cousin also at the school, Paul managed to settle in. And then suddenly it was time for his parents to return to the Kollis.

Seated next to his father, Paul listened with a growing feeling inside him something like having swallowed a hard pit. His father's voice was kind but the words were not what Paul wanted to hear. "Son, you are now old enough to stay in England for your schooling. It is the mission board's policy that children your age be given a good education here at home when they reach the proper age. Thankfully, you will be staying right here with your aunts." Paul swallowed hard. He and Connie would remain with the aunts. His parents would leave in the morning, without them.

Across the room Paul's mother choked on a sob. "I can't bear to think of leaving the children," she said. Tears flowed as she left the room. Paul's father followed her up the stairway. Paul heard his mother's pleading voice, "We can't leave Connie behind. She is only six. It will break my heart to leave them both," she cried.

"They have never been separated," Paul's father said. "Why don't you ask Connie if she would like to go back with us?" Paul's heart beat faster as he thought of losing Connie as well as his parents.

But it was not to be that way, thanks to Connie's loyal heart! His sister had stared at their mother's face with wide eyes. "Oh, Mummy, not without Paul, I couldn't. I could never go back to the Kollis without my brother." The next morning Connie and Paul watched as their parents left for India. They could not watch for long; school waited and after that they would begin their new life with the aunts.

That night Paul read the beautifully painted Scriptures his artistic mother had painted and hung in his room: "I will be a father unto you." "As one whom a mother comforteth, so will I comfort you." Each night he repeated the texts to comfort himself. On Sundays he said the texts he knew in Tamil as the aunts listened.

One year ago on their first Sunday in England, a barefoot Paul had attended the aunts' church in St. John's Wood. Paul had carried his shoes in his hand as was the custom of the Tamil Indians when they attended the little chapel in the Kollis. Now he wore his shoes but he carried India in his heart.

Time went swiftly and Paul moved on from the small private school to the junior-level school. He did not try to fit in. He disliked studying, and the reports that began to come to the aunts seemed to waver between poor to fair and back to poor, to weak, from that time on. Finally a discouraged Aunt Eunice decided Paul needed discipline.

Aunt Eunice had no trouble looking prim but a slight tremble around her mouth gave her away as she tried to appear stern. "Now, Paul, you simply must do better at school. If your headmaster says you can do better then you surely can." With a firm hand on Paul's shoulder she turned him to face the kitchen wall where a small stick now hung on a nail. "If you do as you should we shall not have to use that." In spite of the threat of discipline Paul's school reports were little better. Aunt Eunice managed to use the stick twice, and Aunt Hope urged him to try harder and pay attention.

One thing did help Paul. The thick packets of letters from India, letters his father had written weekly and sent by way of steamship, brought Paul close to his father and all that was going on back in the Kollis. And though they now always contained a gentle note reminding Paul that he expected better from him in his studies, his father's love was strong and comforting to Paul. The letters were also full of the wonders of the forest and mountains his father loved to share with Paul and Connie, and soon became a means for Paul to do well in public speaking class.

Carefully Paul read and re-read the letters packed full of the wonders of the jungle and forests of the Kollis. Today he had decided on the one with a story about the enormous panther that had tried to steal one of the mission's young goats. When it was Paul's turn to speak he began "Let me tell you about the largest panther ever seen in the Kolli Mountains of south India." The class at once became quiet and Paul held his fellow students captive as he went on to tell them about the panther, adding to the story other facts of life in the Kolli forests. For a little while Paul almost felt himself back in the Kollis, a good feeling. As he returned to his seat his classmates' remarks, "Well-done, old chap. Good stuff," followed him. Their words made him feel even better. The letters were an endless resource and speech class, along with reading became Paul's favorite subjects.

Unfortunately, the books he loved to read were not the school books but stories of high adventure. His next school report was still poor enough to make the aunts shake their heads. Hoping to help him, the aunts fixed up a basement room where Paul and Connie could work on their projects. Paul liked science and doing scientific experiments in the basement room, until the day an experiment exploded. Flames shot toward the ceiling causing panic. The frantic maids threatened to quit, and Paul's scientific experiments came to an end.

It was safer to build things, and Paul turned to using skills his father had taught him. "Think they'll like it?" he asked Connie who stood nearby holding the two white mice ready for the new house Paul was finishing. The removable roof was on and Paul stepped back to admire the large two-story house he had just built for their pets.

"Great," Connie agreed. "What's next?" Connie was always ready to assist Paul in whatever he decided to do. This time it was a pair of wooden stilts so high that to reach them Paul had to go through a first-story window. After that Paul made a design for a canvas-covered canoe.

"You can help with the sewing," Paul directed, "and I'll make the frame." When it was finished Paul stood admiring their canoe, with Connie at his side smiling in spite of her sore fingers from all the rough canvas she had sewed together.

But when the mail came later that month with the headmaster's school reports Aunt Eunice frowned, and Aunt Hope sighed. Paul's report read "disappointing," "poor," "weak," "often late." Connie looked at her beloved Paul, worried that he would never pass.

A Cancelled Furlough

Paul surprised himself and Connie when the end of the school term came and he did pass. The feeling that he ought to be ashamed for not trying hard struggled inside him with the knowledge it had been so easy to pass anyway. Paul listened as Aunt Eunice and Aunt Hope heaped words of praise on Connie whose reports, as always, glowed with words like "excellent" and "outstanding." Suddenly the idea popped into his mind that somehow he was a misfit in the family. They were in the parlor and Paul could see his grandfather's fine paintings on the walls. He knew his aunts were considered good poets, and his own mother could paint and draw well. Connie too wrote poems. But Paul couldn't think of anything he excelled in other than getting into trouble.

Thankfully, there were the cousins, many of them, and Paul got along well with them though he hadn't known even one of them before he and Connie arrived in England. The day was mild, the sky gray as Paul searched the sports field for his cousin, Norman. "Over here" he called, spotting Norman standing by himself waiting for him. Paul hurried to join him before the classes began to line up. Norman spotted him and came running toward him. "You still game to sneak off to the Heath?" Paul asked, keeping his voice low.

Norman, only a head taller than Paul and just as lean, nodded. "If we go quickly no one will even notice we're gone, unless of course you would rather stay for some rousing sport?" Norman grinned knowingly. Neither of them liked school sports and had found great ways to avoid them.

Paul's only comment was "Ha" as he led the way behind a nearby shed. From there they could slip into the trees and soon be well out of sight. Paul's heart raced as they began running to the spot where the tallest trees stood. The joy of climbing filled him; the bark of the trees scratching against his bare legs felt good. Climbing was a part of him, something he could never forget. England could not offer all that the Kollis had given Paul in his childhood, but at least there were trees in Hampstead Heath, and it felt wonderful to climb them. High in an old oak tree Paul looked down at his cousin and patted the wide limb beside him. Norman nodded. He too liked climbing and took every challenge Paul gave him.

By the time they were ready to leave for home both of them were covered with black smoke that stained their clothes. It was always the same, no clean mountain air here, just air that left its stain on the trees and on the boys. "Norman, how come your mother who has thirteen children doesn't mind you coming home with more dirty clothes, and Aunt Hope and Aunt Eunice are really put out with just mine? Don't answer that, it won't help anyway." Paul brushed what dust he could from his sleeves. "See you tomorrow," he said and began running in the direction of Nethania as Norman waved and headed off towards his home.

An anxious Connie was waiting for Paul and opened the door for him so that he could hurry upstairs to wash up and change before the aunts saw him. "Thanks," Paul said softly. When he came downstairs Connie nodded her approval at his clean-up.

"Paul," Connie said folding the fresh sheets of the monthly magazine she and Norman and their cousin, Annette, and Paul put together for friends and family, "it feels so long since we've seen our mother and father, that I can't help wishing we were all together again back in our own house." Her blue eyes spilled tears, and Paul reached a hand to pat her shoulder.

"I know, Connie, but look how fast the years are going by." They were not going fast really, but Paul couldn't think of what else to say. "Before we know it they will be finished with their term and the mission board will send them home to England for a furlough. Mother will hug us to death, and Father will smother us in his long arms, and it will be like they had never been gone." Paul took Connie's small hands in his own and gently pressed them. "Hang in there, Connie. Remember that every day means they are one day closer, and you're making them proud with all you're doing here. I mean it, Connie."

"Thanks, Paulie," Connie said and wiped away her tears. She hadn't called him Paulie, her pet name for him when they had been children running free on the Kollis, since they'd come to England. It was just as well, Paul thought. In this house everybody used proper names.

Somehow the term did go swiftly and once more Paul's school reports came to the aunts who again shook their heads in disapproval. The report ended with Headmaster Lake's signature and the words, "Next term we shall hope for better things." The following term reports continued to say things like "poor, fair, poor, weak. Rather disappointing." Paul no longer bothered to think about them. Instead he read more than ever the kind of books he liked, adventures that let his cooped-up spirit free for a little while. But with summer came real freedom: vacation visiting their Uncle Charlie's large family in Northwood.

Uncle Charlie had decided to become a Presbyterian to the horror of the aunts. At Northwood the children were free to do the wild things Paul and Connie hadn't been allowed to do at Nethania. As soon as the train reached their station, the cousins came running to greet them, but Paul and Connie outran them all in their joy to reach the house and begin their days of freedom. Paul kicked his shoes off at the door and vowed not to put them back on till they had to leave. For six glorious weeks they vacationed at West Runton on England's east coast, climbing, running, and finding soul mates in their cousins, Peggy and Nancy both close to Paul's age.

Paul, now tall and lean with the strong legs of a climber and runner, loved West Runton. This was their fourth summer visit and tomorrow they would leave for Nethania and another school term. Paul pushed his bare feet into the long grass and breathed in the air that seemed fresher here. Beside him Nancy, a year older than he, sat with her legs tucked under her skirt and a thoughtful look on her face. They had just been discussing missions and what each of them thought about Jesus sending his followers to reach the world.

"I guess Connie and I never thought we would do anything else but be missionaries," Paul said. "I don't know what I am supposed to do, or where to go when school ends and I have to choose to go on or not." Nancy nodded. She was a good listener and Paul knew they understood each other's hearts when they talked about Jesus and serving him.

"Maybe it's time to begin asking your father about these things," she said.

Paul saw his aunt in the distance beckoning to him and stood. "I think you are right, and I plan to do that in my very next letter to India," he said. Together they walked back to the house and in the morning Paul and Connie boarded the train back to St. John's Wood. That night Paul wrote a long letter to his parents and listed his questions one by one. Satisfied that he had made a good start he sat for a long while thinking about the future and all its possibilities. As always, before he fell into bed his eyes turned to the Bible verses his mother had printed and hung on his walls and he read them softly, "As one whom a mother comforteth, so will I comfort you...." He fell asleep thinking of the verse. He had no idea that soon this school year would bring a great change to his life.

"Paul, is that you, dear? Come straight into the parlor," Aunt Eunice called as Paul dropped his school bag to hang up his jacket. He hurried into the parlor where both aunts sat beaming up at him. His latest school report lay on the table before them. "Wonderful news, Paul," Aunt Eunice said. "You not only did well you are being skipped two grades ahead. I am so proud of you, Paul. Your father will be so surprised and pleased to hear it. Just think of it, two whole grades!"

Paul grinned. He had done well, and secretly wondered if the wonderful summer at West Runton had reinvigorated his spirit enough to help him through the school year. When his father wrote congratulating Paul it was a grand feeling. If only it could last. Sadly, it had not.

"Oh, Paul, how can things have gone so backwards for you?" Connie asked. The headmaster's latest reports showed that Paul was again doing poorly. "He says you are not really trying, and worse he's used the word 'lazy'." Connie looked as if she couldn't believe it. "Father and Mother will be coming home on furlough soon, and you just have to do better, Paul."

"Sorry," Paul mumbled. He was, but it just didn't help when it came to schoolwork. "I suppose Father's letters will show his disappointment too," Paul said. The letters did reprimand him in his father's gentle way of scolding, but for the most part they were full of the wisdom his father loved to share, like animal stories and news about the work in the Kollis. Paul was reading the last letter aloud to Connie when suddenly he stopped. "Oh, no, they're not coming home," he said looking up.

Connie's eyes were wide. "But why? Why not?"

Paul read the awful news aloud. "We are disappointed to give up our furlough this year, but there is another man in the mission who needs it more than we do. Looking forward to next year, we think that the first week in March will be the probable time of our setting sail. That will land us home in time for your Easter holidays."

"Oh," Connie said as her eyes filled with tears. "Not another whole year to wait."

Paul laid the letter on his desk. "It's been six years since we've seen them."

"Paul, do you realize you will be fifteen by the time they get here?" Connie said. "I was only six when they left. Next year I'll be thirteen. Oh, Paul, if it wasn't for their pictures I wouldn't remember their faces clearly." Her voice sounded soft and sad to Paul.

"Yes, but there is nothing we can do about it but accept it and maybe think of something to make the time go faster," he said. His mind raced. "One thing we could do is take all the piles and piles of letters from the past six years and make a book of them. That way Mother can use them someday when she writes a book about the mission work in the Kollis." It worked, and immediately Connie's face brightened. She loved to organize, and putting the vast amount of letters in order was something she and Paul could do.

A Father's Final Letter

"That's it for me," Paul said as he brushed leaves and the ever-black dust from his shirt. "No more climbing today, I say. What about you, Norman, you had enough?" His cousin, Norman, who was hunched over with his hands on his knees, didn't bother to look up as he continued breathing deeply.

When Norman straightened up he was almost a head taller than Paul. "Right," he said. "I've had enough for one day and we still have to walk back." School was over and the sky was blue and the mid June air warm. Tired from a long afternoon of hiking and climbing, they walked in silence letting the sounds of the woods flow over them. Neither of them could have expected what the rest of the day held in news for Paul that would tear his heart and his world upside down.

Aunt Eunice stood waiting for him outside the dining room. Paul thought for a moment that she must be feeling sick. Her face was pale and she looked suddenly old. "Come into the dining room, Paul" she said.

As he stepped through the dining room door, Paul felt a surge of fear go through him. Uncle Bertie, his mother's brother, stood at Aunt Hope's side. Both wore the look of having something terrible to tell him. He tried to remember what bad thing he might have done lately. Uncle Bertie cleared his throat but couldn't speak. Aunt Hope held up a yellow piece of paper, looked at it and then up at Paul.

"Paul, we are so sorry to give you this news, but your dear daddy has gone to be with Jesus." The cable in her hand read, "Jesse taken to be with the Lord after blackwater fever for two days. Break news gently to the children. The Lord reigneth."

Paul heard no more though he knew they were speaking words. He cried out and tried to move but everything in the room including himself was frozen. It was Uncle Bertie who shattered the icy air around Paul when he said, "I must go to Guilford and break the news there." Connie was visiting at Guilford. Hours later, Uncle Bertie came back with Connie.

Paul had gone to his room, shut the door, and sat down on the edge of his bed unable to grasp what he knew he had heard. How could the father he loved and looked up to, his strong, loving, wise, happy father be dead? An hour later the door opened slowly, and Connie came to sit down next to him. Her eyes were wide and frightened, but she did not cry. Paul felt as if he was in a bad dream that he couldn't wake up from. For a while they sat in silence.

When Connie spoke at last in a small thin voice, she said, "It's awful, isn't it." Paul only looked at her. What else could she say? What words could he say? Neither of them would find words that fit their stunned grief for weeks to come.

How could his father be dead? For six years he and Connie hadn't seen their parents, and the letters from home were all they had, and through them their father had gone on being their father, alive through his letters. Because of the slowness of the mail the letters from his father continued to arrive! Tears ran down Paul's face as he held a letter from his father that had just arrived. Written before his father's death, it had only now reached England by steamer from India. Paul wiped away his tears with the back of one hand, sniffed, and continued to read aloud to Connie.

The letter dated May 13, 1929, said, "Yesterday when I was riding over the windswept hilltops around Kulivalavu, I could not help thinking of an old hymn that begins, 'Heaven above is deeper blue; flowers with purer beauty glow.' When I am alone on these long rides, I just love the sweet smelling wood, the dear brown earth, the lichen on the rocks, the heaps of dead brown leaves drifted like snow in the hollows. God means us to delight in his world. It isn't necessary to know botany or zoology or biology ....Just observe. And remember. And compare. And be always looking to God with thankfulness and worship for having placed you in such a delightful corner of the universe as the planet Earth." Connie too was weeping as Paul folded his father's letter and placed it with the others.

A letter from their mother told of the grief of the people of the Kollis who helped to bury their father in a grave not far from the mission house. Paul and Connie were worried as her letters continued to come. Their mother sounded so unlike her old self, and there was no hint that she planned to return to England. "She isn't coming home," Paul said one day looking up from the letter in his hand.

"What can we do?" Connie asked, but it was a whole year before the family decided to do something. At last Uncle Bertie's oldest daughter was sent to India to bring her home. Paul looked at the picture of his mother in his room. She was beautiful, tall, and smiling in the picture. He had been a nine-year-old boy back then, and now he was fifteen years old! Paul looked at his big feet, his hands, the face staring back at him in the mirror. Would his mother recognize him?

The usual crowds of people filled the dock watching as the ship from India came into port. Paul stood next to Connie straining to see the passengers coming down the gangplank. He remembered his beautiful mother as she had been, laughing, full of joy, and though she would look sad now, he would know her at once. His cousin came down first, and then Paul saw his mother! He could not believe his eyes. Grief had turned her into the little, shrunken, old lady that came toward them crying and holding out her hands to them. It was his mother, but not the mother he had once known!

Connie cried "Mother," went to her at once and sobbed in her arms. When it was his turn his mother had to reach up to kiss him, and Paul felt himself rigid with shock that she was so changed. His mother's words didn't help.

She wept often and spoke over and over of her worthlessness now that she was alone. She would never be the same again, she would say, now that the light had gone out from her life. Inside Paul a small root of rebellion and misery poked its way into his heart. Paul couldn't understand the change in his mother and he couldn't seem to help the irritation he felt even when she only meant to help him. As his mother regained her strength she began to take a strong interest in overseeing Paul's last year of schooling. Over and over she talked to Paul about India, and the great need for the gospel there.

She reminded him of India's unreached peoples, so many of them yet to hear about Christ. He saw the shining in her eyes as she told again how she and his father used to sit looking out over the five mountain ranges still waiting to hear the gospel, and how they longed to win them all for Christ. A thrill ran through Paul's chest as he thought of India his real home. Once more his old desire to be back on the Kollis filled him with longing. What was his mother saying now?

"You can go on to school, Paul. Your uncle has offered to pay for medical school. Your father always hoped you would become a doctor and care for the people in all the ways we couldn't with our one year of medical training. There's…"

"No, Mother!" Paul heard his own voice far too loud and lowered it. "I will never be a doctor. You know I hate all that. Anyway, I've had enough of school too." He didn't know what he would do but he was certain about what he would not do.

His mother had stopped talking, but the look in her eyes told him it was only for now. She was far from through.

That very Sunday a guest speaker spoke at church and Paul felt the hair on his neck tingle. "This is Mr. Warwick, a fine builder, and a grand man of God," the pastor said introducing the tall broad man who stood at the pulpit. "We call him Pastor Warwick and I'm sure you will too." Paul sat spellbound as the man began to speak using illustrations right from his builder's experience. Paul thought of all the mission buildings his own father had built, clinics, little schools, the chapel, their own house in the Kollis. When the service was over, Paul didn't see who invited the man to lunch. But the next thing he knew he and Mr. Warwick were walking to Nethania.

At the dining room table Paul sat next to Mr. Warwick and listened to his every word. Tools, building, stories, all of the talk made Paul think of his own father again. "If you would like," Paul said as the meal ended, "I'll show you some of my tools." With

Mr. Warwick's large hand on his shoulder the two went down to the basement workroom.

"You've done a good job, my boy," Mr. Warwick said. "You have a way with the tools and building things just like your father did." The words went straight to Paul's heart.

Back upstairs when Paul and his mother were alone, Paul couldn't help his own words from spilling out. "I want to be a builder, Mother." His mother's eyes sparkled as she listened to Paul. She had a plan! Before the day ended Mr. Warwick and his mother quietly agreed that one of the things Paul would need to learn as a missionary was the building trade. Mr. Warwick would take Paul on as an apprentice.

Paul could barely believe his ears. "If you're willing, lad, to start at the very bottom in the office learning everything a builder ought to know, then you are welcome aboard," Mr. Warwick said before he took his leave of the family.

"Yes, sir, with all my heart," Paul answered. "I can start any time, sir."

Mr. Warwick nodded. "Good, then we'll see you at the office Tuesday morning. Here's the address and my man will meet you there at seven-thirty sharp." Mr. Warwick handed Paul a printed card, and left. Overwhelmed Paul watched from the front window as the great man strode down the street. Next week, he, Paul would stride down the very same path.

The next surprise came to both Paul and Connie. Their mother was going back to India to the mission work. This time Paul felt glad for his mother's decision. His heart was already singing with the idea of working under Mr. Warwick. He would miss his mother but the old resentment and rebellion were gone. One day after he became a builder he would join her in India as a missionary. For now he would live at Nethania and be an apprentice to Mr. Warwick and learn building skills from the bottom up!

Life in Two Worlds

Paul wasn't fully awake but something was shaking his shoulder and someone was calling his name. "Get up, Paul, or you'll be late for your first day of work." Connie stood over him and shook him again as she had been doing for the last two minutes.

Still half awake, Paul finally rolled over and opened his eyes. "What time is it?" he asked.

"Way past five-thirty and you still have to dress, eat breakfast, and catch your train," Connie answered. Paul was up in a flash. He would barely make it. The train ride took an hour and he had no time to lose. "Thanks, Connie. I'll get an alarm clock and set it from now on." Connie shook her head as she left the room. How would Paul hear an alarm clock when he could barely come awake at that hour even with Connie shaking him and begging him to wake up?

Connie was right. The next day and the day after and for almost a week, Paul didn't hear the alarm and it was Connie who came to turn it off for him day after day, shaking and calling him until he awoke.

"No more of this, Connie," Paul said one morning as a tired Connie stood yawning over him. "Tomorrow I don't want you to wake me under any circumstances.

I've got to do it on my own." The next morning Connie listened to the alarm go off, and wonder of wonders within seconds Paul had turned it off. Then she heard him rustling around and knew he really was awake. By the end of a week Paul would wake up as soon as the alarm clicked just before it began ringing. It was a small victory and soon bigger challenges would begin.

Paul already loved tools and building things, but Mr. Warwick was true to his word and first came books again, studying, listening, watching, practicing new skills as he worked in the builder's office. As an apprentice he had to learn things a builder needed to know about contracts, costs, keeping the books, even surveying and its uses. He studied hard, but now his old attitude toward schoolwork and studying disappeared. This time he wanted to know all that went with being a skilled builder. "It feels right" a tired Paul told Connie at the end of his first month. "I feel like I'm really following our father's footsteps."

"I know," Connie agreed. "He loved to build things. And when you are a missionary in the Kollis you'll need to know how to build most everything too."

Quickly the days flew by and at last Paul was sent to work on a building site. Training on the job was great, and he was earning a weekly pay check! Paul knew his work was as good as any of the other men's, but by the second week at the job he was still the "outsider." Lunchtimes Paul sat on a piece of old concrete block eating the lunch Connie had packed for him. Around him the men ate and drank and talked, but not to him. Paul's hands were beginning to look like those of the rest of the men on the crew, broken nails, dirty, roughened. But it was the talk, the way the men spoke that marked him as an outsider. He just didn't speak the way they did. All the laborers spoke what was called Cockney English, thick guttural sounding, sometimes slurred, a way of speaking among them that was barely understandable by those from a social class a step above the common laborer. Paul was determined to be one of the men, speech, clothes, all of it! Within weeks he knew enough to begin sounding like them. After a while, except for the swearing they used so freely, he was truly one of the crew. He had entered their world and could speak freely to them.

On his return home each evening to Nethania where the old, socially right Paul was expected for dinner he entered a world altogether different from the one at his job. It was Connie, loving, faithful Connie who saved the day. Each evening she waited at the door for Paul's return from work. The aunts were upstairs and the house quiet as Connie carefully opened the door and ushered Paul inside. She led him quickly upstairs and while he washed and did his best to erase the signs of a day at the building site, she gathered up his dirty laundry for washing. To the aunts' eyes, Paul appeared at dinner to share tales of his day and looking none the worse for working as a laborer.

"It's a good thing that you have the weekends off," Connie said as they walked one Saturday to watch a cricket match a few blocks from Nethania.

"If it wasn't for you getting me off to work and sneaking me back in every evening I don't know what I would do. Can you imagine Aunt Eunice or Aunt Hope taking one look at my filthy clothes or the mud on my boots, to say nothing of the dirt all over the rest of me. At least I'll be moving on to the joiner's shop soon and I'll also have architectural drawing in evening school coming up too." Paul could feel a surge of energy as he thought of the progress he was making, and soon would come plumbing and then learning masonry. "It's good, Connie," he said. "I can't wait to get started on the next step."

On Sundays Paul taught a Sunday School class of little boys. Looking around the room at the boys, some whispering together, others dreaming of something, and one or two watching him to see what was coming, Paul felt his heart swell with joy. This too was something he loved doing. "Okay, boys," he said, "how many of you like camping out?" Every hand in the room went up. It was not long before Paul began work on the idea of camps for youth fellowship, and he was soon working with a boy's camp. Before he knew it he was also taking on preaching assignments.

Paul was to preach at the St. John's Wood church, and Aunt Eunice felt a trembling in her chest at the very thought of it. "We shall just have to show a brave face no matter how it turns out," Aunt Hope comforted her. "He's only eighteen, and no one should expect too much."

Aunt Eunice moaned. "If only we could count on that. Oh, dear, if only we could count on Paul. One is never sure what that boy will come up with." When the day came both Aunt Eunice and Aunt Hope listened to Paul's sermon, a bit fearfully at first and then with expressions of awe and joy on their faces. He spoke to them about how God was truly all important and his grace more than enough for each of them. Paul was ready to live by this truth. "I think it's time he started to think about going to the mission field," Aunt Eunice whispered. Aunt Hope beamed. They would start right away to encourage him to do that very thing.

Others like Paul's cousins, Norman and Nancy, had already begun urging Paul to think about leaving the building trade. "Isn't it time you took this talent you have for preaching and teaching back to India?" Norman said. They had just come from the Sunday School where Paul had continued to teach his class of young boys every Sunday for the last four years.

"I've prayed for guidance," Paul said, "and I think you are right. It's time I went to the mission field. When I opened the Bible last night it went right to 'I have chosen you for my kingdom and glory.' I'm sure that I'm ready to pick up the work my father died doing in South India. I plan to apply to the same mission board."

Paul hadn't planned on being rejected by that very mission board. "We're sorry, son, but we don't think you are ready to go to the field, and so we are rejecting your application at this time." Paul could barely believe what he had just heard the head of the mission board say to him. How could this be when he'd prayed for guidance and it seemed clear that God wanted him on the mission field? He listened quietly to the list of things the mission board felt he still needed to do.

At home Connie was waiting for him, and Paul shook his head as he handed her the rejected application. "Not ready, the board said. They want me to do more preparation and then apply again."

"Oh, Paul, this says they want you to take a basic course in medical training." Connie's blue eyes glistened with tears. "I know how you hate blood and all that, but basic medical training would be good to know back on the Kollis." Her voice softened. "I'll be leaving soon to attend Mother's old school for a year of basic tropical medicine. Maybe you ought to try applying there too."

"I thought about it on the way home," he said. "I'm glad for you, Connie, but I've already made up my mind to go to the one the mission board suggested, actually the one father went to, Livingston College, for a course in hygiene and tropical medicine. It will mean working at a local hospital doing dressings in the wards and learning the principles of diagnosis and treatment. That shouldn't be too bad." He had no idea that it would be life-changing.

A World Upside Down

Paul hurried through the hallway of the small local hospital where he'd been assigned as part of his year's training in medicine at Livingston College. He was on duty tonight in the emergency ward learning to do dressings and tend wounds. A new patient had just been wheeled in on an ambulance stretcher. Paul stood against the wall to let it pass. "Accident victim," one of the attendants said. "She's lost a lot of blood, don't know if she'll make it."

The young woman on the stretcher looked as still and deathly pale as a white marble statue. Her eyes were closed and there was no response to those who tended to her. Paul was sent running to bring the equipment for a blood transfusion. He returned quickly and watched as nurses swiftly set up the transfusion. Other patients arriving in emergency needed attention and Paul was ordered to watch by the young woman's bedside. A steady supply of blood flowed into the young woman's vein and almost at once Paul noticed a faint tinge of color touch the woman's skin. Soon lips that had been deathly white began to turn pink. Astounded by the effect of the blood transfusion, Paul stared at his patient and saw a faint fluttering of her eyelids. He was still watching intently when she opened her eyes and asked for water! Paul felt his heart gripped by the miracle of shared blood that had brought the young woman back to life. Once he had hated the sight of blood when as a young boy he watched his missionary father cut away infected flesh, but now he saw the life giving power of blood! The wonderful way God had made the human body fascinated him and by the end of his year of training he had fallen in love with the field of medicine. To the great joy of his mother (who did not say, "I told you so") Paul decided he should go to medical school and fulfill his father's dream for him to be a missionary and a doctor.

Paul took his uncle's offer to pay for medical school and entered University Medical College. With his arms full of books and his head full of lectures, Paul's days were filled once more with studying and learning, and he loved it. "This is where I should have been all along," he wrote to Connie. Why had he wasted four whole years learning the building trade? Had he missed God's guidance somehow? He could only shake his head and groan at the time he had let slip by him. What neither he nor Connie could have dreamed was how much those four years becoming a master builder were to play a major part in his life's work.

It was September 2, 1939, a day Paul, like all of the students and teachers alike, would not forget.

Their country was at war with Germany! It wasn't long before Paul and the other medical students were sent out of London to Cardiff for safety. Paul and his roommates stayed in a large boarding house run by a Mrs. Morgan, an older woman who carried a large hearing aid, a horn, everywhere she went. She ran a strict house and that included morning prayer meetings where she would go from student to student to listen as they prayed. It was Mrs. Morgan who kept pointing out to Paul the fine qualities of a certain young lady medical student, a Miss Margaret Berry, a doctor's daughter.

"Margaret is a bright young woman and loves the Lord. She'll make a fine missionary wife," Mrs. Morgan shouted to Paul as he left the breakfast table. Paul already knew he was interested in Miss Margaret Berry. Paul smiled at Mrs. Morgan and shouted his thanks for the good breakfast. Right now he had other things on his mind, like the war news which was not good.

The London Blitz had started setting whole sections of the city on fire. Night after night the German bombers came, and Paul was soon ordered back to London for clinical work in a surgical firm. Casualties poured into the hospital. Like the other medical students Paul worked full duty, on call every night. He tried to sleep between tea and supper after working all day and before the next rounds.

Sometimes he had to make do with only an hour's rest before breakfast.

Operations went on continually. Bent above a hand full of glass shards, Paul marveled at the structure of the hand before him. "I can hardly believe the wonder of the human hand," he said to the nurse assisting him. "What a marvel of engineering," he went on, "there's nothing to compare with what God has done in the hand." The young nurse nodded silently as Paul continued to point out the wonders of muscles and tendons exposed before them.

When the hospital was bombed they were evacuated to another for more surgical and clinical training, and here Paul worked under a doctor known for his great studies of pain. Paul wanted to learn everything he could about pain.

In spite of the war, graduation from medical school was finally in sight for both Paul and Margaret. Paul had made a decision, and wasted no time. "Margaret, will you marry me?" he asked. Margaret smiled, already knowing what her answer would be. They were married a week before graduation. On their honeymoon out in the countryside Margaret had her first climbing experience with Paul, who never lost an opportunity to climb a tree. She was soon following him, learning to climb and beginning what would be a lifetime of learning the joys of the outdoors with Paul. They were sure God had called them to the mission field, but when and how they would get there with the war on was not yet clear.

As the war worsened Paul was desperately needed in London. Days he worked on orthopedic surgery, nights on the casualties of war. Margaret had gone to stay with her parents in Norwood where she could help in her father's clinic. Every other weekend she and Paul tried to spend time together. Paul had never been so busy, and he still needed to go on for his FRCS, Fellowship of the Royal College of Surgeons. "I'll have to study night and day to pass the first part of the test for the FRCS," Paul warned Margaret. He managed to be one of the eleven out of 100 who passed!

While bombs fell and Paul spent the night at the hospital operating, baby Christopher was born. Paul, like most young men his age, was now in military service. While he was still working at the hospital a call came to join the University College Hospital where he could also finish his FRCS. The war office allowed him a year's time to go. Paul passed his exams and qualified for the FRCS in orthopedics with special interest in nerves, hands, and feet. Now there was nothing to keep the army from sending him for duty in the Far East. Not even the new baby he and Margaret were expecting to join them and young Christopher would stand in the way of the War Office.

"If only this new baby would come before you leave," Margaret said, "at least you would see our little one. Oh, Paul, your mother is back on the mission field in India, and Connie is married and already gone to Africa, but it looks like God has other plans for us, at least for now." She patted her stomach as the baby kicked.

Paul put his hand on the tiny outline of a foot. "He will show us the way, my love. There isn't a day goes by, or a night that he isn't watching over us and guiding us."

But God's plan had not changed and that very week a call came for Paul to come and serve at a Christian hospital in India in desperate need of a surgeon. They knew it would take a miracle to release Paul from his army duty.

By the end of the week a new little girl had joined the Brand family, and Paul was packing for Vellore.

"It's only for two years," Paul said as Margaret watched him pack.

"I know," she said, brushing away a tear. "Besides, it's a miracle that the War Office has released you to go to the only accredited Christian Hospital in India." She handed Paul another shirt to pack. "If you don't go they will surely lose their government license to teach all those students waiting for you."

"This is the work we've dreamed about, Margaret. I'll be a missionary doctor in India for two years. It's the beginning, thanks to God and Dr. Cochrane.

The doctor, in charge of the Vellore Christian Hospital in India, and superintendent of the Leprosy Sanatorium at Chingleput, had been a guest lecturer on leprosy at Livingston College when Paul first met him. He had persuaded the War Office to let Paul go.

"Remember, love, it's just for two years, and we know that all the Dr. Cochranes in the world couldn't have opened this door without God's hand."

The day came and Paul left Margaret and the children, waving goodbye until he could no longer see them. Was he leaving home, or more like going home? From the time he stepped onto India's soil, the sounds and smells and sights of India brought back the familiar things of his childhood. He began to pick out words in Tamil.

Vellore was a teaching hospital and the sight of the college grounds surprised Paul with its beautiful garden and stone buildings set in a lush green valley outside the town. He couldn't wait to write to Margaret about the grounds, the hospital's 400 beds, and the house two miles from the hospital and six from the college where he shared space with another doctor and his family.

Paul barely settled in before he was given a heavy load of surgery work as one of only two department head surgeons. Paul covered all the orthopedic cases. Hundreds of patients came daily. In his letters home Paul described his work, "I am working longer hours here than in the London Blitz, and have more difficult cases." In another to Margaret he wrote, "It is the hot season and I am operating in 110 degree heat. We dare not have fans in the operating room and yesterday I soaked one gown after another. I am taking plenty of salt, but my body is covered with prickly heat. The

Indian assistants tell me my body will adjust by next year."

His letters home were now full of excitement about his love for teaching the students and his patients.

"Margaret, my dear one," he wrote, "I am convinced that here is where we are to serve the Lord. You and the children must come as soon as you can."

On the day Margaret arrived after a long, hot journey with the two children, all three tired travelers were suffering from prickly heat, boils, and dirt. Paul enveloped them in his arms, dirt and all. Though they would return home to England on furloughs, India would be home to them for almost the next twenty years.

Chingleput

Margaret and the children settled into their new home with a happy Paul. His family was with him and he was at last doing the work he loved. Paul's students were awed by his operating skills and his patience with them, but they loved his good humor. Often he would set them to laughing as he acted out the symptoms of one of the many illnesses they needed to know about, and then asked them to diagnose the problem. During an operation he would ask things like, "What is a surgeon's most important tool when blood starts spurting from a puncture?" He would demonstrate the answer was one's thumb, by having a student press his thumb on the area. Paul loved teaching, but even more he loved his patients.

Shy patients soon learned they had nothing to fear from this gentle doctor who listened to them. He was also re-learning Tamil to speak to them, studying the language in spare moments. At a patient's bedside his kindness showed and those who went to chapel learned about the Jesus Paul loved and followed, and who also loved them.

When Paul's old friend, Dr. Cochrane, insisted he come visit the work at the leprosarium he headed at Chingleput, Paul went. No hospitals would treat lepers at all and isolated clinics and roadside dispensaries did what they could. Chingleput, helped by the British Mission to Lepers, was well run under Dr. Cochrane, with sturdy buildings, grounds well-kept and lined with trees and flowers. Paul was glad to see the lepers busy growing food, making cloth bandages, keeping the gardens and shops, doing whatever they could. "You know," Robert explained as he led Paul across the compound, "the sullphones we give to treat them help, and the disease burns out. But, as you can see, they still look like lepers, even when they are no longer contagious, and always will, which makes them outcasts wherever they go."

Paul remembered his childhood and his father's careful tending of a handful of lepers, not touching them with his hands and forbidding Paul and Connie to go near them.

Robert went on speaking. "No eyebrows, no noses to speak of, clawed hands or stumps, and no feeling in their hands or feet. Do you know there are ten million lepers worldwide, and two million here in India?"

Paul had stopped to watch a young man take off his sandal. Neither his thumb or fingers would work. At once, Paul, the surgeon, wanted to see those hands. He hurried over to the man, said he was a doctor and asked to examine his hands. The fingers were curled under like claws, and Paul carefully pushed his hand under the clawed fingers. "Can you squeeze my hand?" he asked. Immediately Paul felt a terrible strength squeezing his hand unmercifully. "Stop!" he yelled. Wringing his injured hand, Paul comforted the young man. "I know you could not feel your fingers squeezing mine, and you had no way to tell how hard they did. What it means is that not all of your hand is paralyzed."

As Paul and Robert walked on, Paul began to think out loud. "Why do fingers and toes wear off? Could surgery help make a claw hand usable?"

"You have a lot of questions, Paul, and there is a lot we don't know yet, but I can tell you now that no one does surgery of any kind to straighten a leper's hands. Some badly infected parts have to be amputated, or diseased bones removed, but never repairs. No orthopedic surgeon has even studied the deformities of lepers."

Paul stopped, stared at Robert, and demanded, "How can that be? We worked on hands during the war and we know a lot more now than we ever did. And you are telling me that no one is doing anything for millions of people with deformed hands? Why hasn't it been tried?" By the end of the day Paul could think of little else but the needs of both the souls and bodies of these lepers. He needed to find out everything he could about leprosy. There had to be a way to help them. The first big question was simply to find out if a leper's flesh was so bad it could not be operated on. Do toes and fingers rot away and fall off? He began reading everything he could find on leprosy. Days he worked 10 to 12 hours, spent time with Margaret and the children, and studied. Weekends he went to Chingleput to hold hand clinics.

Others at Vellore helped Paul with the tests and x-rays he brought back from the two thousand patients he examined at Chingleput to look at every paralyzed muscle, thickened nerve, and absorbed finger. At last the pattern was clear that in every case it was the same order of muscles that paralyzed, and the same order of those that stayed strong. Now Paul knew there were good muscles he could use to replace paralyzed ones.

Not even Vellore Hospital would take in leprosy patients for fear of frightening away other patients, even though the disease did burn out and the evidence showed that many adults were immune to leprosy. But Paul finally got permission to secretly bring in a few leprosy patients to an isolated ward hidden from the rest of the hospital.

"We will start with a patient whose hands and feet could not possibly be made worse," Paul said. Krishnamurthy, the young Hindu boy before him, a volunteer from Chingleput, barely lifted his head as Paul spoke to him. When he did, Paul saw in his eyes only despair and hopelessness. Cast out by his family, shunned by all, his life had become that of a beggar, refused all shelter, all transportation, all employment. He had come to Chingleput hoping only for food.

"Do whatever you want with them," Krishnamurthy said in a dull voice, holding out his clawed hands and gesturing towards his feet, twisted so that he could not walk straight. Paul and the nurses quietly smuggled Krishnamurthy into the secluded ward of the hospital set aside for Paul's new leprosy patients.

On the day of the operation, his first attempt at reconstructing a leper's feet and hands, Paul prayed silently as he looked down at his waiting patient. Would the operation be a success, or would those who thought he was wasting his time to work on a leper's bad flesh, somehow turn out to be right after all? "Are you ready?" he asked.

Paul gently took Krishnamurthy's hand. Both hands were useless claws that could barely pinch things between the side of the index knuckle and thumb. But today it was the boy's feet Paul would operate on first. The large ugly ulcers on the soles of both feet were deeply infected and the bones were showing. The young Hindu boy looked up at Paul and nodded. "Well then, Krishnamurthy, let's see what we can do to fix those feet," Paul said.

The operation was a success and Krishnamurthy recovered enough so that Paul could begin work on his hands. Then came long hours of therapy to exercise the newly connected fingers and learn to use them. The smile on Krishnamurthy's face as he began to see his thumb and fingers working landed right in Paul's heart. By the end of a whole year in the hospital the repairs were finished and they worked! Krishnamurthy was no longer the young man who had come to Paul cast out of his family, out of society, hoping only for food to live. But for months he had wondered, why did these nurses and staff, the doctors treat him with such love and care? He had begun to listen carefully to the chapel messages about their Jesus.

When Dr. Brand spoke of the forgiveness of Jesus, the Son of God, who had died for his sins, and the new life, the eternal life Jesus offered to all who would come to him, Krishnamurthy's heart at last understood. With tears he listened to the good news and asked the Lord Jesus to save him. While Paul and the staff watched, Krishnamurthy was baptized. "Now that I am a child of God, I wish to be called John," he said.

"A good Bible name," Paul agreed, and from that day Krishnamurthy was John. Paul knew that no matter how difficult the terrible prejudice that surrounded leprosy was, his fight against it was worth it all.

Meanwhile Paul's family was growing. First baby Mary and now little Estelle. Paul made time to play with the children, and young Christopher had already learned to be a climber like his father. With the help of Indian ayahs to tend to the children, Margaret began treating patients with eye disease. Half a million of India's people, many of them children, suffered blindness from cataracts.

At Vellore Paul's skills as a surgeon were gaining a reputation that was already reaching places like England. "If only I could see how the nerves are affected," Paul said aloud to his assistant, "but I need a body for that, someone who has had leprosy."

"Ah, but you know that is not the Indian way. You might work on a cadaver but you must do it in secret and sew it back up before anyone would find out." A week later a call came. There was a body being held in a shed several hours away in Chingleput. If Paul came quickly he could work on it for a few hours. Paul and his helper left immediately. That night by the light of a lantern Paul saw the clear pattern leprosy made on the body's nerves. The disease caused the nerves to swell near the surfaces. Now Paul and his team knew what they needed to add to their careful record keeping.

Dawn was beginning to light the sky as Paul and his helper stitched up the last incision in the body and covered it over. A tired but excited Paul drove back to Vellore, where again the stigma that surrounded his leper patients had found another victim.

Krishnamurthy, now John, was back at Vellore. One look at him made Paul wince. John looked defeated. "I cannot find work. Everywhere I go no one will hire me, no one will allow me a place to live. They see my face and know that I am a leper. It does not matter that I am cured." He held up his new hands, "and with my hands no longer looking like claws I cannot beg enough to live on."

"But John, you know how to type." Quickly Paul sent up a prayer. "And I'm in need of a typist. You will fit right in." John did fit in well, but there were so many others like John, their leprosy cured and no longer a danger to anyone. They needed work, places to live, and ways to set up a cottage industry in their own villages. Paul began thinking and praying and sharing his dream of a place, a kind of factory, school and living area to meet those needs. When an elderly American patient gave money to build such a place Paul couldn't wait to share the news with Margaret.

"Think of it, love," he said, "The buildings will be small, mud-walled, whitewashed, and grass roofs on them, but we'll have a trade center, a place to teach the proper use of tools for a leper who can't feel his hands."

Tears glistened in Margaret's eyes, but they were tears of joy. "Oh, Paul, let's be sure there are flowers and gardens too. They could learn farming skills and caring for fruit trees too," she added.

"We'll call it *The New Life Center*," Paul said. "They can make things that they could one day do on their own. How about toys and puzzles? We could sterilize them for marketing." In his excitement Paul's dream grew by the minute.

Margaret laughed and reached for his hands. "Paul, look at your hands," she said. "Do you remember when you used to think those four years you spent learning the building trade were surely a waste? It never was,

Paul. God meant these hands to repair bodies and more. He knew you would need to know the skills of an engineer, how to plan, and how to build this place."

"You're right, Margaret. Even in the operating room at times I've used something from my plumbing days to point out a good technique to my students." Paul grew quiet for a moment, and his eyes seemed to Margaret to see something far away.

"Margaret, I don't think God ever wastes anything we put in his hands," he said softly.

It was one of the few quiet moments Paul would have for a long time.

He worked days at Vellore, weekends at Chingleput, and between teatime and dark at the New Life Center. Somehow he still found time to play with the children, and tell them the stories they loved.

The New Life Center now housed and trained lepers who came from all kinds of past lives. Some had been wealthy, educated, others poor, illiterate and now they shared living and learning new lives at the Center. The markets soon welcomed the fine toys made at the center and sterilized for sale. But something else was happening at the center that would help turn the world's thoughts about leprosy upside down. Paul's doctor's eyes and ears were beginning to make discoveries that would change the lives of his patients even more.

Cuts and Blisters, Rats and Cats

As word spread that Dr. Brand could operate and make new hands for lepers, more and more patients were coming and asking to have operations on their hands. The seventeen beds in a remote corner of the hospital were constantly full; The New Life Center flourishing. On the table in front of Paul and his team lay stacks of records, months of measurements, notes, drawings with details of patient's fingers and toes that kept track of every small change. "It's been a mountain of paperwork, but this is the proof that we are on the right path," Paul said. "We can see the effects of leprosy on faces, hands and feet, but we still don't know how it causes the shortening or loss of fingers and toes." Paul rubbed his forehead wearily and looked about him at his faithful team. "You've done a good job, all of you. We have strong evidence right here in our records that leprosy doesn't cause bad flesh like most of the world still thinks. If it did our operations wouldn't last. The repairs would be impossible on bad flesh." His team murmured agreement.

Paul lifted another packet of notes and held it high. "And right here we have evidence from the cadaver we spent a whole night dissecting and recording, that shows us the patterns of nerve damage."

"Yes, doctor Paul," one of his newest staff members said, "and we know leprosy damages nerves and it destroys the feeling in hands and feet, but how does it do that?"

Paul shook his head. "That is the mystery, son, that we have yet to solve" he said. "It's always been a doctor's aim to relieve pain but now we know the lack of pain, of feeling is far worse. Our patients don't feel it when a thorn is cutting through a foot to the bone, or the heat of a metal pot is burning his flesh. But thanks to our research we do know fingers don't fall off, they are hurt, infected, and shortened from outside causes, 99% of the time. Our records are proving it."

Paul selected another record. "This record alone shows a man who has lost fingers and toes over the past five years, though he was cured of leprosy six years ago, before he lost a single finger or toe." Paul placed the paper on top of the others. "Leprosy does not cause bad flesh, and we are proving it."

The young man nodded. "So, we must continue to track every scratch, every mark, every change in our patients and find the causes," he said. "And keep the records!" he added.

"Right! And lads, and lasses," Paul said, "there are a whole pack of detectives waiting for us at the center. Those boys are becoming experts at reporting things and finding the culprits for their own wounds." The job was, Paul thought, to convince every patient to do so.

Sometimes a boy didn't want to own up to something he'd done that caused his wound. It was evening inspection at the Center, and the boy standing in front of Paul held up his hand to show the deep cut between his thumb and index finger. He tried to look innocent as he answered Paul's question. "I can't think of anything that did that. I just worked with my spade as usual, and there it was tonight when I looked."

"Really?" said Paul. "Let's go take a look at the tools used today." Sure enough Paul's hunch was right. The lad had forgotten to take his own spade with him to work and used an old one he found at the site. The handle of the old tool had been wrapped in wire and enough wire loop stuck out to have irritated the boy's hand. Dark stains on the handle were clear evidence of what had happened.

The boy hung his head and confessed. "I didn't want to go back for my own tool, but I never felt the wire or I would have stopped using it."

Paul gently touched the lad's shoulder. "Of course you didn't feel it, son. That's why you need to inspect every tool you use carefully before you start work." One day later Paul was faced with a far more difficult case. During the night a large part of another boy's finger had simply disappeared.

"It was there last night," the boy said as tears filled his eyes. "I don't know what happened." Paul swallowed hard. If a finger did fall off it would mean they had failed in their observations. Inch by inch Paul and the others searched the room.

"There, Sahib," one of the boys called, "I see blood." In a corner of the room a small bit of dust and dirt and blood told the story. Rats. During the night a rat had come and bitten off the boy's finger. No leper patient would have felt such a thing. Paul sighed deeply, and then it came to him. He would find the kind of cat they needed to keep away the rats. From then on cats were the favorite pets at the Center. When a patient was fully cured and trained and able to return to his village, Paul made sure he left with a kitten of his own.

Soon another strange puzzle faced Paul and his team. Some of the patients were finding blisters on the back of their hands each morning. None of the blisters had been there the night before. This time careful detective work and observing the night routines turned up the culprit—the reading lamps. Each night those patients who liked to read would grasp a small knob on their lamp to turn it off when they were through. The lamps gave off a great deal of heat. Because not one of those who read at night could feel the heat as their hands brushed against the hot glass they burned the skin without knowing it.

Paul knew exactly what to do. Using his builder's skills he fashioned large square knobs that could be turned without the hand touching the hot glass. It was one of many times Paul used his builder's skills. Tools needed to have large handles easy for his leper patients to grasp. Nails had to be held with pliers as they were pounded. Often Paul simply sat and watched the men in the center work. Every problem had to be solved to keep them safe from the pressures and wounds that were the real causes of bone shortening and infections that brought the loss of fingers and toes. If only they could feel pressure but they couldn't. Their hands never felt the encouraging hand of a nurse during an operation; their feet never felt a nail sticking through a shoe into the flesh. The leprosy could be cured but it left them permanently without the protection of pain that a normal person felt from a hot stove, a sharp knife cut, a blistered heel. Paul longed to help his patients live new lives. He loved them and wasn't satisfied to see just repaired hands and feet. To be declared cured of leprosy wasn't enough. Paul wanted them whole, body and soul and spirit. But not every patient cooperated, at least not the teenage boys who came into the center full of boasting how much they could do with their unfeeling hands. When asked about a new wound, they would shrug and say, "Oh, leprosy does that." The excuses fell flat, but Paul was patient. In time boasting of how much they could do with their painless hands turned into a competition at the daily inspections to be the best at having kept their hands and feet fully inspected and free of new damage.

Paul loved them, even the boy, John Karmegan, who seemed bent on making Paul, the staff, and everyone around him miserable. He had come to Vellore with leprosy so severe that little could be done for him surgically. Margaret stitched the boy's eyelids half shut to save his sight, and Paul did the only other thing he could do for John by providing a place for him to live and be fed in the New Life Center. John hated how he looked and the world around him for the cruel way it had treated him. He stole, lied, cheated, was mean to other patients, and even tried to stir up trouble like getting others to go on a hunger strike against hospital rules he disliked. Paul prayed often for John and continued showing him the love of Jesus through his patient care for him.

The love of the staff and other Christian patients at the Center seemed to have no effect on John. One of the nurses shook her head as she reported the boy's latest tricks to Paul. "I think we cannot rehabilitate this one," she said. Paul was beginning to wonder himself. And then Paul's mother came for a long visit.

Granny Brand, as she was known among the patients felt drawn to John. She spent time with him again and again telling him about Jesus' love for him and showing him the way to become a child of God. One day, when the two of them were talking, John began to weep. He wanted to accept Jesus into his life. He was baptized in a cement tank on the grounds while Paul and staff and other patients watched with joy.

John had friends now among the patients, but he wondered if Christians outside the hospital grounds would accept him even in the local Tamil church. His grotesque face looked the same awful way leprosy had left him in spite of his new life. Paul took the challenge and called the local church, assured them John was no longer contagious and asked if John could come and take communion though they used a common communion cup to drink from. The church leaders said "yes" and so breathing a silent prayer that no one would show John rejection, Paul took him to church.

As a trembling John stood at the back of the church, a man raised his head, smiled at John and patted the seat next to him. From that day on John knew the joy of being one of God's children, accepted in his family. Years later, on a trip to a Vellore factory now employing lepers and disabled workers, Paul was taken to meet their best employee who had just won the all-India prize for excellent workmanship. The beaming employee was John!

Once again Paul felt a great joy in God who had guided his feet from that first visit to the leprosy colony at Chingleput to work with the despised of the world, those thought hopeless, like John.

"Paul," Margaret said one evening, "I thought God would send us to India someday because India was always in your heart, but I didn't dream we would end up working with lepers. Each time I treat a leper patient's eyes and he doesn't go blind because of cataracts I'm so thankful." The children were in bed and a cool breeze fanned them where they sat enjoying the quiet.

Paul breathed in the night perfumes of India's flowers planted in the nearby gardens. "Connie and I used to tell each other that someday we would do just what our missionary mother and father did in the Kollis. And here we are both missionaries, Connie in Africa, and the two of us here in India." Paul turned to look at Margaret. "No, I never dreamed of working with lepers, and now I dream of little else." He held out his hands and stared at them for a moment. "What a marvel of engineering God has done in our hands, Margaret. When I operate on a patient's twisted fingers and find a way to bring them back to usefulness, I know God is pleased."

Margaret gave a happy laugh. "From the number of all the operations ahead of you, I'd say he will be very pleased."

Paul was operating the very next morning and had just finished when an attendant came with the news that Paul's mother had come and she was not alone. Slipping into fresh clothes he hurried to greet his mother. He was halfway down the corridor and could already hear her familiar voice insisting that "her son would certainly take in the three leper patients she had brought with her." Paul knew the few beds available were already full but he also knew his mother's determination. She was still trekking through the Kollis to reach remote villages. She brought them the good news of Jesus, treated the sick, started schools and gave little thought to her own wellbeing. When she'd fallen off her pony too often, she'd hired a boy to help her. On the trails she camped in a tiny, homemade tent wrapped in netting. Her wants were few and small she insisted, except for one, her determination to take the gospel to the unreached people of the Kollis.

"Mother," Paul greeted the little old lady whose wrinkled face beamed up at him.

One look at the lepers she had brought by cart, by foot, by train, and Paul knew once again his mother had delivered some of the very worst cases she could find. Her faith in God and in Paul was strong. Paul smiled and greeted each of his new patients, already noting their claw hands and bandaged feet with his surgeon's eyes. They would find beds somewhere.

I was a Stranger

Paul's research had taken him away for several days, and Margaret didn't expect him home for another three days. She had been in the garden and the young man standing near the house seemed to be waiting for her. As she drew closer there was no mistaking the clear signs of leprosy.

"Please, I am looking for Dr. Brand. I was told he might help me," the young man said. He looked barely able to stand. On one hand most of the fingers were missing, and his thin sneakers were dark with wet stains of what were surely weeping ulcers on his feet. Margaret knew by the red rimmed look of his eyes that he was already nearly blind.

"I am so sorry," she said, "but Dr. Brand is away. He will be back in a few days. If you stay in Vellore until then I'm sure he will see you." The young man thanked her and began walking away on legs trembling with fatigue. "You will find a place to stay, won't you?" she called.

He turned to look at her and shook his head. "No, I don't think so. The hospital would not let me in. The bus driver turned me away and I had to walk here."

It was already evening, and Margaret knew the youth had probably not even eaten, and from the look of him he desperately needed a place to rest. "You can come home with me," she said firmly. "I can make you a bed on the porch and bring you food there until Dr. Brand returns." As he followed her to the house, Margaret remembered every warning Paul had given her to keep the children from contact with patients who were contagious. Though most adults were immune to leprosy even when the disease was in its hot stage before the disease was cured, children were less immune when exposed.

When Paul came home Margaret quickly explained about the young man staying on their porch. "Why did you do that, Margaret? You know the danger to the children."

"Oh, Paul, how could I turn him away when my morning Bible reading had just reminded me that Jesus said 'I was a stranger and you took me in.'" Paul hugged her tight. "The verandah was a good idea, and I know you kept the children away. There is always some risk, just remember, love, to take all the precautions you can." He was soon hurrying to greet the young man, Sadagpan, his new patient.

For Paul and his staff, taking precautions in the operating room and out of it was a way of life. It seemed a certainty that most adults were immune to leprosy. Dr. Cochrane at Chingleput thought so too. In all his years of working with lepers none of the staff had ever gotten the disease. But no one knew for sure that they were immune to leprosy. An accidental finger prick while working with a patient whose leprosy was not yet cured meant examining your own finger for any signs of the disease. Paul examined his own pricked thumb often, but the truth was even he thought less and less about catching the disease as he cared for patients.

Paul left Sadagpan settled in his new hospital room. As he passed another of the patient's rooms he saw Namo, one of the staff, sitting at the bedside of an older patient. He was working on the old man's fingers. Paul lifted a hand in greeting and smiled. "Thank you, Lord, for that man," he whispered. Namo, a former patient at the hospital, often amazed him by the work he did now with his own reconstructed hands. Sometimes his loving care brought results Paul had not thought possible.

When Namo had first come to Vellore, he felt he had nothing to live for. Hopeless and angry at people's cruel attitudes toward lepers, he'd come to Paul wanting only to do something for other lepers. The loving staff at Vellore took him in. Paul operated on Namo's hands until they were restored to usefulness. Each operation had been followed with therapy. Under the patient love and compassion at the New Life Center, Namo had become a brother believer in Jesus Christ. Now he was a fine therapist helping other patients recover.

As he left the hospital and walked across the warm sunny grounds, Paul remembered Namo's first case.

A nine-year-old boy whose clawed hands were badly damaged and stiff had come to Vellore for help. Paul had known he could not restore the child's hands. He remembered telling the child, "I'm sorry, but the damage is too great. I'm afraid all we can do is fix those rigid fingers into a useful position."

But Namo had begged to try therapy with the boy. "Please, Sahib, let me first try to help him. I will work with his fingers every day. "And Namo had. For three months he rubbed the boy's fingers with oil and exercised them for hours each day until Paul saw a slight improvement. He'd allowed Namo to keep working with the child. Patient, loving Namo worked with the boy's hands for a year-and-a-half. The results still melted Paul's heart. The fingers were supple enough for him to operate and restore the boy's grasp. And Namo had never stopped his loving faithful work with the patients.

So many patients came that Paul now had to make hard choices. When a blind man begged him to fix his hands so that he could play the organ, Paul felt sorry for him but sure that he would never play the organ well. "I want to bring music to people," the blind man pleaded. Paul couldn't refuse him and did operate. The day finally came when Paul was invited to hear the man play a small organ that had been brought in. The first sounds were so bad that Paul groaned. But suddenly the notes began to come together and the beautiful music of "Amazing Grace" filled the air and Paul's heart.

Other former patients now worked at Vellore as social workers, record keepers, and in staff positions. Before their hands had been restored such work would not have been possible. Paul lay awake at night thinking of new ways, better ways of operating to help his leprosy patients. And soon the word of the work at Vellore spread far enough to catch the attention of the Rockefeller Foundation. The Foundation wanted to help Paul with his research by sending him around the world, anywhere he wanted to go to talk with other experts, take all the time he needed and they would pay the bill. Paul could barely wait to share the news with Margaret. He would visit and study the techniques of the world's best plastic surgeons and hand surgeons! Though not one of them operated on leprosy patients, he was anxious to learn all he could for use with his own patients. And this was the very chance he needed to talk to the experts who studied nerve damage. No one yet knew the reason for the pattern of swollen nerves he and the team saw in every autopsy done on cadavers of lepers. God surely had sent this offer from the Foundation.

"Oh, Paul," Margaret said putting down an armful of children's toys to hug him tight. "We're due to go on furlough, so this grant couldn't come at a better time." Once more Paul and Margaret and the children left to travel to England where Margaret and the children would stay with the aunts, while he began his research. The aunts were ready for Paul's little family and had set aside a large room for the children's use. Margaret tried to smile, but knew that this visit would try the aunts' patience sorely. It wasn't long before someone passing the house hurried in to report a child hanging ten feet above the ground on a lamppost bar. Young Jane had repeated the very thing her father and Aunt Connie had done years before her at Nethania.

Paul had to cover his laughter at the astonished neighbor's look. Like his father before him, Paul let the children learn the way he and Connie had by trying things. Already he'd treated Christopher's, and Jean's many scrapes and sprains. They needed strong bodies and minds, but he was far more interested in the health of their spirits and souls. "Have a grand time with your mother and your aunts while I'm gone, and mind them well," he said. His plans included heavy research in England that would take him away for some time.

"Don't forget, Daddy, that I'm to be the hero of the next story when you come back," Jean urged him looking up with solemn eyes. Paul made a habit of inventing long stories where his characters were the children. Usually he gave them a part quite the opposite of their natures just to keep their interest. A timid child might be facing a fierce tiger at the edge of a cliff, or something equally daring.

"Don't you worry, young lady. I'm already thinking," he assured her.

Paul spent the first part of his research trip in England observing the best hand surgeons. He spent time with many and talked about his own work with leprosy patients, and was even asked to lecture about his own work. It was his lecture to an important group of plastic surgeons that brought him to an honor he never expected.

"You must present your paper on the reconstruction of lepers' hands to the Royal College of Surgeons as a Hunterian lecture." Paul had just been invited to receive the Hunterian Professorship, an honor given only once a year and the highest honor in surgery. Paul could not believe the chance to speak to these men, but more than the honor he wanted the chance to open their minds to the work that could be done with lepers, the things he and his team were proving at Vellore.

When the day came to give his lecture, Paul was instructed about the ceremony he must attend. First he was given a formal welcome by the president of the society at tea, and after that dressed in the traditional red gown of the society. Paul was led into the lecture hall by a silent procession of red-robed members. No one introduced him and at a nod from the leader, Paul began his lecture. When he finished he was led behind the leader in another silent procession from the hall. Afterwards there was a celebration and Paul received the honor of Hunterian Professor of 1952. It had been a humbling experience but one Paul knew could open doors to interest in the leprosy work at Vellore. As he left the city of London Paul didn't dream that in 12 years he would be back, once again with red robe and all to receive a second Hunterian Professorship, this time for his work on reconstructing lepers' feet. Paul left England for the next lap of his research. He had seen many of the best doctors and picked up good techniques but not one could answer the question of how to bring mobility to stiff fingers.

For his next four months of research Paul went to the United States while Margaret and the children left England to visit her folks in South Africa. He began with a visit to the only leprosarium left in the United States, the Public Health Service Hospital in Carville, Louisiana. His reception at Carville was less than warm; a taste of the opposition Paul would face more and more as he shared the findings of the rehabilitation work at Vellore. Paul's words on his work with lepers at Vellore were greeted with polite applause. The director of Carville had heard all he needed from Paul to strongly disagree with Paul about the effects of leprosy. "We thank you, sir, for coming," the director said. "We agree that injury and stress may cause damage to patients' hands. But I've been in this business a long time, and I can assure you that Hansen's disease itself causes these fingers to shorten." Paul would hear words like those over and over. The Americans also chided him for saying leprosy instead of Hansen's disease, the name of the doctor who had first discovered the bacilli that caused leprosy. Paul left Carville that day unaware that God's plan would bring him back one day to head the work of rehabilitation at Carville.

Paul traveled next to Boston where he hoped to see a certain nerve specialist well known for his research using cat nerves. Paul had brought with him specimens of nerve damage from his leprosy patients. As he laid them next to those of the Boston doctor, Denny Brown's specimens of damaged cat nerves, he was amazed. They were identical! "Your leprosy patients' nerve damage happens when the leprosy bacilli invade the nerve, inflammation starts, and the nerve swells. The cat nerves were damaged by a different irritation but the pattern is exactly the same. The nerve swells against its sheath and cuts down the blood supply," Dr. Brown said. This was Paul's first clue to the swollen nerves he and the team had found in leprosy patients. It would prove in time to lead to the reason for paralysis in lepers' hands: the cutting off of the blood supply would cause the nerve to die. A dead nerve could not carry signals for feeling and movement.

Paul was finally back home at Vellore with Margaret and the girls, his Rockefeller trip behind him. As Margaret served them all marmalade tarts and tea, Paul seemed lost in thought. "What is it, love?" Margaret asked nodding to the children who were ready to run back out to play.

Paul watched the children running madly towards the small playground. "Do you know that outside of the hand surgery we do here in India for our patients, there was only one other surgeon doing surgery on lepers' hands, only one in all those countries. And, Margaret, not even one expert has ever studied leprosy-damaged nerves. If it wasn't for Dr. Denny Brown's cat studies we still wouldn't have a clue what causes damaged nerves in leprosy. As for noses it was almost as bad. I found one nose surgeon who had ever worked on a leper's nose." Paul turned in his chair to face Margaret. "What we are doing here at Vellore is pioneer work in this battle. And it is a battle."

"Yes, love, but this is God's work, a battle for souls and minds and bodies, to give our lepers hope and new life."

Paul ate one of Margaret's delicious marmalade tarts, his favorites. "I could almost laugh at what the head of one leprosarium in South Africa told me. After I'd lectured and shared our findings here, he was still not convinced. I pointed out the blisters on the palm of one of his patients and told him they were most likely from burns he hadn't noticed. Do you know what he said?"

Paul deepened his voice and swelled out his chest. "Sir," he said, "I've been in this work all my life, and you just a few years. I tell you leprosy causes blisters in the palm of the hands." Paul shook his head. Margaret smiled and Paul reached up to take her hand. "We will keep on battling until even the World Health Organization decides we're right and gets behind the fight to make rehabilitation for lepers a worldwide dream come true."

Paul sighed. At least another dream was coming true right here in India. While they were away on furlough, the Indian government had given a large tract of land to be used for the work in leprosy. At last Paul would have a whole hospital of beds for his leper patients, a rehabilitation center, and even research labs. At the moment it was desert land, treeless, hot, empty of trees, but it would become beautiful, a place for the treatment of lepers unequalled anywhere. "Yes," Paul said, "and we can thank the Lord for the new center, Karigiri."

Margaret nodded. "With your dear friend, Ernest, heading it we can thank the Lord for a double blessing. Do you know he has already ordered hundreds of trees and plants? With the new watering trenches and systems I think Karigiri will be transformed within the year."

"Cut them off, Sahib"

Paul had given new hands to Sadan, the young man Margaret had let stay on their veranda, but nothing seemed to work with his feet. Toeless, shortened to small rounded stubs, large red deep ulcers covered the soles of both feet. Nothing Paul and his team did helped, though they tried penicillin, creams, ointments and everything available.

"Do not waste your time," Sadan said. "Go ahead and cut them off below the knee. It is what other doctors would have done before I came to Vellore."

Paul had just changed Sadan's dressings for the tenth time. His love for the gentle Sadan was breaking his heart. Perhaps the other doctors had been right. He might have to amputate because he could not stop the terrible infection from the ulcers. "Sadan, it makes me sad, but soon we may have to amputate after all," Paul said. Sadan bowed his head and Paul saw the tears running down his face as he nodded that he understood. Gently Paul led him to the door and watched him walk down the steps and head towards the road. Astounded, Paul gasped. Sadan was putting his full weight on the exact spot where he had just spent an hour cutting out infected flesh and cleaning a terrible abscessed wound on the ball of his foot! No wonder the wounds never healed.

"Wait, Sadan," Paul shouted. "I know what is wrong with those feet and it's not bad flesh." Paul explained to Sadan nothing would help heal his wounded feet because they were not being allowed to heal. Leprosy patients didn't limp on a fresh wound because they never felt the pain that causes normal people to limp. Instead of amputating Sadan's feet Paul and his assistants encased the cleaned wounds in plaster casts. The feet healed. The news spread to other leprosariums and finally the number of amputations among leprosy patients fell dramatically. It was all part of the proof Paul continued to fight for: leprosy did not cause bad flesh, and rehabilitation was possible. But healing Sadan's feet was only the first step. Next came preventing ulcers in feet that could not feel pressure, irritations or wounds.

"What else can we do?" Paul said, as he and the team once more studied the records of their patients' feet. "We've insisted on everyone's wearing of shoes, but the problems are still not going away." He held up one of the patient's charts. "This man wore his shoes all day and never felt the tiny metal screw that dug into his heel. He noticed only that night when he saw it imbedded in his heel."

"There must be a way" one of the team said, "to protect their feet."

Paul nodded. "We must keep trying. This morning I ordered chairs and benches to be placed throughout the grounds so that our patients can sit and rest their feet." Neither Paul nor his staff realized that no amount of sitting would help. After years of research they would finally understand that the very act of walking was the main enemy! It was walking itself that exerted a force on a leper's foot that started the chain of dangers leading to the terrible ulcers.

Leprosy patients simply walked, never noticing a blister or any other pressure from a shoe. Eventually an ulcer formed and if infection set in and was not healed with rest, tiny pieces of bone fragments broke off and oozed from the wounds. This could lead to loss of toes and even a whole foot. Meanwhile the leper would feel nothing and would not even limp.

Paul and Margaret were now working with the Mission to Lepers, though Paul also continued to be professor of orthopedics at Vellore. On one of Paul's many visits to other leprosy work he found a doctor in Kano, Nigeria who agreed shoes might be the answer to preventing ulcers. Together they worked on making a special shoe. At a shoe company near Kano, Paul found a tennis shoe with an inner sole that could be molded to fit a patient's foot. With a soft lining and canvas outside it was still cheap enough and might work. Preventing the foot from bending while it moved, and spreading the pressure by molding the shoe to the foot were a must, but the softness of leather was missing, and the shoe soon caused blisters.

Paul and his staff began experimenting with all kinds of soft materials, starting with sponge rubber. Sadan, their willing helper, patiently tried shoe after shoe, wearing them until sadly new ulcers appeared, signaling that this latest shoe was not yet right. Patiently Sadan would say, "Some day we will win." Neither Sadan nor Paul knew how long the search would take.

In India Paul took his problem to the Bata Company, a big shoe manufacturer in Calcutta. The company agreed to mix rubber to different degrees of softness for Paul to test. Back at Vellore, the entire team now wore strangely shaped shoes as they all tested shoes of different thicknesses. After a year they settled on a mixture for softness that seemed best. But the right kind of shoe was still a problem. A friend working in prosthetics became interested and visited at Vellore to help Paul. "Leather, not plastic," he said, and so began the search for a leather that could be molded to the patient's foot. At first the shoe worked! But Paul found that a leather shoe was just not strong enough to take the rough use it would get in places like the muddy paddy fields of South India.

When a young man, John, came to Vellore wanting to work for Paul, he soon found himself making shoes in the work shop now at Karigiri. John found a way to make the rubber used even better, and it was John who helped Paul design "rocker" shoes and boots.

The foot needed to rock like a seesaw on a pivot instead of bending in order to prevent too much pressure on the foot. To solve the problem two small rigid parallel bars of wood or very heavy leather were placed under the sole of the shoe. This was the shoe that Sadan wore for years without a trace of an ulcer on his feet! The only problem seemed to be that a patient could more easily turn an ankle, even fracture it without knowing, and continue walking. A high boot to support the ankle helped, and Sadan now wore the high boots. But another problem soon came because the boots were so expensive.

"Alright," Paul said as the team discussed the problem of cost, "we know that wearing even a simple sandal can help. We need to catch patients with their first ulcer and teach them never to go barefoot and what to look for continually to prevent another ulcer." Paul decided to send teams into the villages around Vellore to teach leprosy patients what they needed to do. Amazingly, the number of ulcers was soon reduced by half.

Paul and the team were thankful for the results but they knew that the right kind of shoes was the best solution. A leper needed good shoes to prevent ulcers and damage to his feet even after his leprosy had been cured for years. Without the warning signal of pain to help them, lepers were in danger of damaging their feet for the rest of their lives. They needed the right kind of shoe. All over the world Paul's work with lepers was beginning to be known and shedding new light on one of the darkest diseases of mankind. But age old customs and ideas stubbornly remained even in India. For one thing, Paul's patients needed shoes, but they also needed to be convinced that they must wear them faithfully. Back in the Kollis to visit his mother, Paul saw the urgency to make sure patients understood what they needed to do.

While visiting his mother, Paul also wanted to travel to the village home of Karuninasan, one of his former patients. Paul's mother, all of five feet, had to look up to her tall son as he saddled her small hill pony for the trip. Though she was well past retirement she still traveled the hills picking up unwanted children, seeing to their education, preaching the gospel, opening schools, tending the sick, and on occasion bringing the worst cases of leprosy to Paul. Karuninasan had been one of those cases.

"I'm so proud of Karuninasan," she said, shading her eyes from the sun. "He is the only man in his village who can read, and he has started a night school. He works hard days in the fields, but every Sunday he rides his small pony to our church here in the village."

"Yes, Mother, and thanks to you who brought him all the way to Vellore for help, he can use his hands and feet to do all those things." Karuninasan had come to the hospital with paralysis of both feet and hands and large, ugly ulcers on his feet. It had taken a year for all the operations and healing to happen.

"Thank the Lord, son. Karuninasan is a fine Christian man now," his mother said.

Paul turned once to wave goodbye as he headed toward Karuninasan's village. He could hardly wait to see how his former patient was doing with his reconstructed hands and healed feet. He especially wanted to see how the carefully fitted, molded shoes so lovingly made for Karuninasan in the Karigiri shoe shop were doing.

Karuninasan saw Paul coming and came toward him holding up his hands in the traditional Indian greeting. "Sahib, welcome. I heard you were in the Kollis visiting your mother."

"Yes, my friend," Paul said tethering his horse. "News travels fast even in these hills. It is good to see you."

"Come see the school where I teach now." Sahib's face was lit with joy.

Paul hugged him warmly and stepped back. All he could think of were the bandages on Karuninasan's feet. "Why are your feet bandaged?" he asked. Paul didn't wait for an answer. "Please sit down here, and let me see them." Carefully Paul unwrapped the bandages. On both feet terrible sores had deepened until the bones showed through them. "Oh Karuninasan, what has happened? Where are your shoes?"

"Sahib, I have them still" Karuninasan said. "Come let me show you." Paul groaned as he watched Karuninasan walk on his unfeeling, horribly wounded feet. He took Paul into his small house. "They are there," he said, "on the shelf." The shoes were wrapped in brown paper and as he undid them, Paul saw a pair of shoes looking as new and beautiful as they had back in Karagiri when Karuninasan first received them. "You see, Sahib, how I have kept them from harm. Each Sunday I wear them when I go to church."

Paul shook his head and patiently began all over again with Karuninasan. It would take tending to the ulcers, plaster casts, and rest to heal his feet, and thorough training so that they stayed that way. Karuninasan would not again go barefoot.

The days passed quickly and Paul was once more on his way home to Vellore. Thinking of Karuninasan's barely worn shoes he frowned. Paul knew he could have fashioned a pair of shoes right there in the Kollis had Karuninasan's been worn out, but he had never expected to find good shoes just sitting on a shelf. Shoes and how to make them for lepers had filled his mind and heart, and his teams, for so long in the search for the right one, they even dreamed about shoes. "But if our lepers and the rest of the world could see what a difference shoes could make in keeping wounded feet like Karuninasan's from happening it would make the years of work here worth it," he thought. As soon as he was back home he must write another paper for publication on these things. Groaning, he thought of the heavy schedule waiting for him. Writing, lecturing, operating and researching took much of his time. Thankfully, some of the students trained by him were now working at Vellore and Karigiri using the skills and techniques he had taught them. Invitations came to him from all over the world to lecture. His thoughts went back to the many poorly equipped leprosariums he had visited where old views of leprosy and bad flesh were slow to change. He had battled for the truth many times, and the light was slowly starting to come to such places.

Back at Vellore and Karigiri, Paul and his team were hard at work on the problems cured lepers faced. "We need to find better ways to take away the signs of leprosy from our patients' faces as well as their hands and feet," Paul urged his team. People's fear and shunning of lepers hadn't gone away in India or the rest of the world yet. Not even a certificate showing their cure could make a leper accepted in most places. A face without a nose and without eyebrows was a well-known sign of leprosy. "Our patients need eyebrows and noses. Those are hard areas to reconstruct, and so far we haven't done very well in that department."

"I've read that there are some new ways of doing skin grafts for burn victims that grow hair and can be transferred to the brows," one of the young staff offered.

"Good for you," Paul said. "I'll be observing surgeons this month who are among the best in that kind of operation. Once we know the right techniques we'll try them here."

The operation worked and soon Paul was using the new techniques to make eyebrows for his patients. The operations did so well on one of his patients that the man's new eyebrows grew thick and bushy with long hairs. Paul always advised his patients to keep the new brows trimmed, but this man was so thrilled with his black, bushy eyebrows he would not trim them. He returned home proud of his new eyebrows which were truly the bushiest, longest-haired eyebrows in the village. One of the marks of leprosy had been erased. Others like rebuilt noses soon followed. Even a truly large nose that looked like a nose should was welcomed by his patients.

Paul's days were so full that he was always glad for the times of just sitting with Margaret after the children were in bed. "Think of it, love," he said as they shared the evening breezes together. "Our lepers' faces will never be beautiful, but with eyebrows and noses they're finding work in the villages. People are beginning to accept them at the markets, in the streets."

Margaret's eyes glistened with tears. "It has taken a long time for the truth about leprosy to be known. I'm so glad God planned for us to be here doing this work, Paul. So many of our patients have found faith in the Lord, and now new ways to serve him."

"God did plan this for us, in spite of the fact that being a doctor was the last thing I used to want to be." Paul rose and took Margaret's hands. "And you, my dear, never treated eyes once before coming here to India. Now look at you, an eye specialist treating hundreds of cases." Margaret laughed and stood close to Paul. Together they watched the sun go down until only shadows remained and the last bird calls faded. The night air carried sweet smells of jasmine and pungent spices.

"I've almost forgotten what an English garden smells like," Margaret said.

Paul laughed and touched the tip of her nose. "But at least you have a nose and quite a perfect one," he said. These days Paul looked at noses with a surgeon's eye. His view of a perfect nose had little to do with size or beauty. It was God's marvelous creation, something he and the team did their best to imitate for their beloved lepers.

See for yourself, Sir

"Do you have company at your house today?" Margaret overheard a young friend ask one of the children.

"No," was the quick answer. "I mean, yes. Daddy is home today." Margaret shook her head. Paul traveled so much for his work these days that his visits home might indeed make him seem like company to the children.

Paul swung his little daughter high in the air. "Company, am I?" Gently he put her down and watched her running off to play. "Margaret, love, I have good news. Do you recall the Marconis, the movie producer and his wife from Bombay? He's agreed to make a short film of our team's work in leprosy."

Margaret's face turned from surprise to sheer delight. "Paul, that's wonderful! Seeing what can be done will spread the news even better than just hearing of it."

Paul nodded his head. "In all this time we've reached so few. There are leprosy workers out there who haven't heard of our ideas. World leprosy conferences have done nothing on the subject of making new hands and feet for lepers. This will be a chance to see clawed hands transformed! The film will cover our work here and the New Life Center, and true cases rehabilitated. The Marconis have invited you and the children to Bombay while we work on the project."

For six weeks Margaret and the children and Paul stayed in Bombay. Tricia, who was three now, especially loved the Marconi's pet leopard cub, Gigi. The cub loved her back. When their stay was up Tricia reluctantly left her friend, Gigi, behind. The Marconi's first film titled "Lifted Hands" became a great success. And Paul asked them to make a second film of an actual operation at Vellore, one Paul could take with him on their next furlough to show surgeons in England. This one entitled "Tendon Free Grafting" brought tremendous applause at its showing, and later won several film awards.

The time had come for a furlough and Paul was excited. "Margaret, I can't wait," he said holding a packet of letters in his hand. "Can you believe this, I'm invited to show the film on surgery to the British Orthopedic Association. Just think of it! At last a tool we can use to show what can be done for lepers."

"Yes, dear" Margaret replied. "And I'm looking forward to time with family who need to see our own little brood." All of the Brand children were eager to go, and like their father before them it would be an adventure not to be forgotten. Sadly, at its end both Christopher, fourteen and Jean, twelve years old would stay behind in England, just as years ago their father and Aunt Connie had been left behind in England to finish their schooling.

Paul and Margaret were headed back to the work they both loved as official staff members of the Mission to Lepers. But Margaret and the three little ones were a bit quieter on the trip home without their beloved Chris and Jean, and Paul did his best to cheer them. "Margaret, will you ever forget the look on that customs officer's face when he asked you what was in the bag you were carrying?"

"Oh dear," Margaret said, "I thought he actually turned pale when I said it was just toys some lepers had made in India." She laughed and the children laughed and then they were all remembering funny incidents at the aunts' house in Nethania.

Paul wanted to see the Marconis in Bombay on their way home. As they drew close to the Marconi's home, little Tricia spotted her old friend, Gigi, chained to a stake near the house. Only now the leopard was full grown. Before Margaret could hold her back Tricia ran to pet her friend. In an instant the leopard had knocked the little girl down and sunk her teeth into the child's throat. The Marconis quickly came to help Paul force the leopard's mouth open and release its grip. As the leopard was led away Paul helped his daughter up. "Let's get you cleaned up. That Gigi is playing too rough." A stunned Margaret watched as Paul took little Tricia's hand and led her to the house. Paul's calmness had its effect and other than a few small scars Tricia was soon fine.

Back at Vellore Paul was busier than ever. For the first time the World Health Organization decided to sponsor a ten-day conference on the work being done at Vellore. Surgeons and people in leprosy work, heads of organizations for the disabled, important people from all over the world were coming to Vellore. Paul and his team displayed their years of photographs following each patient's case. For most every patient there were at least 36 photographs of hands and feet showing conditions before and after operations and following them through therapy. Every case had been carefully documented, and the years of proof that rehabilitation for lepers was a reality lay before the visitors. For many visitors it was an event that truly changed their views. "I had to see it to believe it" some said. And they did believe!

Paul and the team also displayed their years of research on shoes for lepers. They still needed to do more study of the effects of pressure on the foot. The rocker shoe they'd made was good, but new machine technology was helping them learn more in the search for the right shoe. They already knew that any repeated pressure could cause damage, much like a continual clapping of hands becomes painful. A leper could not feel the pain that could warn them of danger, but neither Paul nor anyone else had yet found a good way to signal a patient of too much pressure. Paul was so busy with the visitors that he barely saw Margaret and the children. "As soon as this conference is over I promise we'll have a vacation. We'll all go spend Christmas with Granny Brand up in the Kollis. We'll bring our own Christmas dinner to share. How about taking a big, fat turkey with us?" Four excited little girls began immediately deciding what else should come with the turkey, what presents they should make for Granny Brand, and all they might need for the trip.

The trip to the Kollis began with a one-hundred-and-fifty-mile drive by van and then twenty more miles by jeep across rugged roads to the foot of the mountains.

Granny Brand had sent a pony and two small dholis for the steep fifteen-mile climb up to the small mountain settlement where she lived. Paul and Margaret with children, luggage, and a fat-stuffed turkey arrived at Granny's little house in the midst of schoolboys who waved colored banners on long poles to welcome them.

The girls couldn't wait to show Granny the fine turkey. "Yes, indeed, that is a grand, fat bird," Granny agreed. "We will save him for dinner tonight. This noon we are having rice and curry with all the workers and their families right here on the grounds."

"That will be just fine," Margaret said quickly. She had seen the disappointed look on Patricia and Mary's faces. "We will have a lovely picnic, won't we girls?" The magic word picnic soon brought smiles to the children. They were well acquainted with picnics.

The afternoon went by quickly. Paul spent the hours treating patients in the small hospital set up. He had just finished when Karuninasan arrived wearing his shoes!

"Sahib, look, no bandages no ulcers, and almost no shoes left," Karuninasan said and grinned.

Paul could see that the once almost new shoes on his last visit to the Kollis, now looked badly worn. "You have been a faithful student, and worn your shoes well," Paul said. "But you need a new pair, Karuninasan. Shall we go see what we can find and make you a pair?" The two were soon hard at work as Paul cut and shaped from wood and leather a new pair of shoes using what he could salvage of the inner soles of the old pair. The new shoes fitted to Karuninasan's feet brought claps of joy from the crowd of villagers who had come to watch.

As evening fell the children's excitement grew. Good smells from the back room of Granny's house surely meant a Christmas dinner was coming, turkey and all. "But first," Granny Brand said firmly, "our teachers and their families are coming to sing carols and praise the Lord." People were already crowding into the small screened porch and soon the prayers began. On and on the praying and praising went until young Mary began to squirm and in a whisper ask when they were going to eat Christmas dinner. Margaret gently hushed her. Then the singing began, first carols in Tamil and then in English, many, many carols. Pauline was asleep with her head in Margaret's lap. Next to her, Estelle could not keep from yawning, and Patricia could no longer hold up her head which seemed to want only to rest on her mother's shoulder. At last the meeting ended and the family went inside. Margaret only hoped the children were still hungry for the long awaited turkey dinner. "Now what?" she thought as a heavy knocking at the door brought them all to silence.

Without a word, six dark-skinned men entered carrying a sling on poles. Lying in the blanket sling was a woman who looked like she was either already dead or close to it. Silently the men placed the blanket with the woman onto the floor. Granny Brand cried out immediately, "Back, back" The men quickly stepped away to make room for her. Paul was already kneeling by the woman searching for a pulse. His mother nodded as she too knelt and found a faint, feeble pulse.

"It's typhoid," his mother said. "She is dehydrated. Hurry" she ordered, "bring me buttermilk in a bowl and a spoon."

Paul shook his head. "We ought to have medicines but there isn't time to go and find some." His mother had put the woman's head in her lap and was now slowly dripping tiny bits of buttermilk from the spoon into the woman's mouth. As she did she spoke softly in Tamil to her and urged her to swallow. A teaspoon full was too much and choked her, but tiny bits were dribbling down the woman's throat. Another hour passed and still Paul's mother patiently fed tiny sips of liquid to her patient.

"Mother," Paul finally said. "It is getting quite late. Maybe someone else can take your place so you can come have dinner with us."

Paul's mother turned fiery eyes to him. "How can you think of dinner. This woman is dying," she said.

Paul nodded and silently went to Margaret signaling her to help him take the children into the back room. Margaret tried to give each of the girls a bit of the long awaited turkey but mostly they wanted to sleep. Paul helped her put them to bed and went back to sit with his mother and her patient.

Many hours later, Paul suggested that typhoid could be a danger to the children and it might be wise to move the woman to another hut. "You have gotten quite a bit of buttermilk into her," Paul said. "I think you could safely leave her with someone else now to take your place." This time his mother agreed. In the morning the woman was much better. Paul and Margaret would never forget this Christmas night, without presents, without even the turkey dinner they'd hoped for, but with something far more wonderful. They'd seen the love of Jesus brought to a dying stranger by his faithful servant. It would make them smile to remember that at least one of the children had asked the following morning, "Did we have Christmas yet?"

Her Majesty the Queen
Requests ...

"Mother, is it true the Queen is coming to India?" Mary had run all the way from the garden and come to a screeching halt in front of Margaret. "Please, can we go see her, Mother. We could all have a holiday, couldn't we?" she begged.

"No, dear, I'm afraid we aren't invited" Margaret said smoothing her daughter's tangled hair. "One has to be invited to see the Queen unless she is in a parade and you live close by to watch her go by. I'm sorry, but we haven't been asked and we certainly don't live close by. As to a vacation in Madras, it would be nice but your father and I are both busy. Run along and play, dear." Margaret watched her go running past Paul who was on his way towards the house. Many of their English friends at the compound had been invited to the Queen's reception, but Paul and Margaret hadn't received one, and it was just as well, Margaret thought, since she hadn't a thing to wear to such an affair.

Time for the Queen's reception arrived and their friends had left when the phone rang. Paul answered it. "Yes, we'll be there," he said. Margaret saw the look of surprise that crossed his face as he hung up the phone. "You won't believe this," he said. "Somehow our invitation didn't come, but that was a call asking where we were. We are supposed to be introduced to the Queen at this reception. Six couples, and we are one of them!"

"Oh, Paul, what will we wear?" There was so little time, and Margaret had no idea what she would wear, or Paul either. With help from the staff at Vellore, Margaret borrowed a friend's old but serviceable long dress, and found a pair of gloves to go with it. Paul borrowed trousers that were too long and had to be altered, and a suit jacket a bit too big for him, but they would do. There was barely time to make it to their Indian friend, Dr. Ernest Somasekhar's house in Madras and from there to the reception.

"Come in, come in," Ernest said, ushering Paul and Margaret into his house. "Come upstairs with me, Paul, I have a surprise for you." When Ernest opened the door to a large bedroom Paul saw at least a dozen men's suits in all sizes hung about the room. At the surprised look on Paul's face, Ernest laughed and gestured to the suits. "We heard you were having a problem finding suitable clothing for this event, but surely we can find something here to fit you." They found the perfect formal dark suit with matching white shirt in exactly Paul's size. Once again, God had planned all along that Paul would have what he needed for the ceremony ahead of him.

All sorts of dignitaries in fine clothes filled the great room where Paul and Margaret waited with the small group who were to be presented to the Queen and her husband, the Duke. "Oh, Paul, I hope I don't forget everything they instructed us to do," Margaret said.

"Let's see," Paul said, "if the Queen speaks to you, when you answer her you are to say your Majesty after you finish each sentence. If she talks more with you, you may address her as Madam. The Duke is to be called your Highness, or Sir!"

"Yes, and when the Queen reaches out her hand to greet me, I am to touch only the tips of her fingers as I curtsey," Margaret added. It was time and Margaret's heart sank as their name was called.

The Queen and the Duke looked more splendid and royal than Margaret could have imagined. Paul was presented first and then Margaret. She started well, but suddenly began to stumble and would have fallen if it had not been for the Queen's hand. The Queen spoke to them so kindly that Margaret forgot to address her as Madam, or Your Majesty. The Duke recalled meeting Paul before and asked about his work with hands. They were soon talking like two old friends. The moments with the royal couple passed swiftly. Only afterwards did Margaret realize all her mistakes, but in spite of them she had found herself enjoying the Queen!

On the long trip back to Vellore, Margaret went over and over the details of the glittering reception, the elaborate foods, the women's gowns, and of course everything she could remember of their time with the Queen and the Duke. She needed to be ready for four little girls eagerly waiting to hear it all. Paul answered her musings with an occasional "Hmm." Already his thoughts were on the patients, the students, the projects waiting at home. They were close to home and Margaret had stopped chatting, but suddenly Paul's heart overflowed with joy and gratefulness. Ahead of them were the first buildings of Vellore and he could see his beloved New Life Center. "How good the Lord has been to us," he said. "How many of his lost sheep have come here and found shelter, and new life in Him."

Margaret who had been thinking so much of royalty, smiled and said, "I think it is a work dear to his heart to see his people once despised and shamed now lifting their hands to him the King who proved his love to lepers. And," she added, "for many they are hands made new and useful thanks to the skill and faith he's given you, my love."

"For that you get a kiss on your nose, and I shall drop you at the door and go back to the hospital," Paul said. What he didn't tell Margaret was that he needed to go and fetch the fine, fat, live turkey he had ordered for them all. Christmas would be here soon bringing Jean and Christopher home for the holidays. Paul wanted a turkey well fed and cared for and fresh for the Christmas dinner they would have together. Caring for the turkey would be a good project for the children to take on until then. He hadn't counted on Mary.

The day before Christmas Paul overheard Estelle and Mary talking about the turkey that would be made into dinner the next day. "How can you eat a friend?" Mary insisted. "It's not right to eat a pet." Her voice quivered with feeling. Paul smiled to himself. He loved a joke and had just thought of a good one.

The Christmas table was beautifully set with the great covered meat dish in the center. Paul insisted everyone must sit down at once and not keep the wonderful meal waiting. When the grand moment came, Paul swooped the cover off the meat dish and out popped the family cat who made a wild scramble from the table and out of the room. Everyone including Mary laughed at the mighty good surprise joke. However, the turkey had not escaped and proved to be delicious.

Paul's good sense of humor was widely known and his students loved his gentle cheer, often his way of showing rather than just telling them something as he taught. Margaret had grown used to Paul's humor too. So when he informed her that India's Minister of Health was coming to Vellore and wanted to stay with them, she smiled sweetly and said, "Well, dear, since our beds are all in use I doubt she can."

"My dear," Paul joked back, "I can just sleep on the edge of our bed and you and she can share the rest." Margaret aimed the pillow she was plumping at him and chased him from the room. But on the day before the Minister's arrival, Paul once again reminded her and this time insisted it was no joke. She really was coming and was planning to stay with them! Margaret found room for her guest, and Paul wondered if he'd joked just once too often for Margaret.

It was early one evening when the worst of Paul's nightmares came. The telephone rang and Paul heard a frantic voice on the other end saying, "Sahib, come quickly, the New Life Center is on fire! All the boys are out and safe, but you must hurry."

"I'm on my way" Paul said. "Get water and wet down the thatch roofs, and tell the boys they must be careful of their hands. Their lives and their safety are more important than all the Center's buildings." Paul prayed as he ran. "Lord, keep the boys safe." Their hands would not feel the damage of flames and hot metals if they tried to help. The roofs of the huts could catch fire in a moment. But to Paul's relief he found most of the Center's huts still standing. Smoke filled the sky above the ruins of what had been the workshop. Soot covered boys huddled in the courtyard. One walked toward Paul.

"Sahib, it was my fault," he said. "I was working with the plastic sheets for microscope covers, softening them in hot oil over the kerosene stove. The oil pot tipped accidentally and the fire started." Young Rajasakran sounded close to tears.

Paul put his arm about the boy. "You were able to get everyone out and look at your hands, not a blister." As Paul examined the hands and feet of each boy he found not one blister. But all were in need of comfort. "Boys," he said, "in the New Life Center the most valuable part is New Life, you boys, your hands and feet, your faith, your brave hearts. You all showed me tonight that even in an emergency you know how to protect your hands and feet. I am so proud of you." Paul lifted his arm in a sweeping gesture to take in all the surrounding buildings still standing. "And see how blessed we have been tonight. No wind blew, yesterday's rain left us plenty of water, and we have all learned something about working with plastic for the future. Come with me to the chapel and thank the Lord for his goodness to us, for the things we have not lost, and the things we have learned."

What had been lost, Paul knew was the heart of the Center so needed for the rehabilitation of the boys. He had helped to build it and spent many hours there. To Margaret he spoke his deepest pain. "I spent so much time there," he said, "saw so many boys find hope it feels like I've lost a part of me." Paul looked at his hands turning them over to see the palms. "I tell the boys to protect their hands, and now I must use my own surgeon's hands to help rebuild. Thing is," he turned to look at Margaret, "it has never occurred to me that I could injure them and find myself in need of repairs."

"Well," Margaret said firmly, "what you need is a good night's rest. I know you, Paul Brand, and you couldn't keep from rebuilding any more than you can resist a patient with a need for a new hand. Furthermore, I don't think God gave you all those skills for nothing. You'll feel better tomorrow and we'll pray for everything that's needed for a new building."

Not only did money for a new building come in but for a far bigger and better one. And Paul loved helping to plan and put it up whenever he could be spared from the hospital. When the building was finished the boys could now make all the things they had made before the fire and a great many new things including furniture! Paul could barely believe the grand new shape his first dream of a center had taken.

The 5 p.m. Committee

In his office at Vellore's Medical College, Paul stooped to write a note on the daily calendar he kept open on his desk. "Meeting: Building Committee, 5 p.m., home."

Paul's secretary had seen such a reminder many times over the last two months. At Vellore buildings were constantly being built or added to, and Paul's building skills were often called upon for advice. She had no idea of the real meaning behind Dr. Brand's reminders to himself of the 5 p.m. meetings.

At exactly 5 p.m. on Building Committee meeting days, Paul, dressed in an old shirt and shorts, would be standing in his garden surrounded by children. Piles of bricks lay on the ground near a large container of mortar being stirred by Mary and one of her friends. Other children were passing bricks down a line to Paul and his young helpers. They were building a playhouse and Paul was teaching them how. In the midst of all the laughter and fun, Paul was passing on skills to the children much the way his own father had taught him years ago in the Kollis.

Margaret tucked a strand of hair behind her ear and picked up a pair of Paul's trousers from the laundry piled on the floor. Her absent-minded husband often forgot to empty his pockets before tossing them into the laundry basket. Sure enough, a rolled up letter of some kind was sticking from a back pocket. Margaret rescued the roll and opened it. "What on earth?" she exclaimed. "Her Majesty the Queen requests the honor of your presence…" Clutching the notice Margaret ran to find Paul.

"Paul," she cried spotting him in the garden. "This is an invitation to receive an award from the Queen!" Margaret waved the notice in her hand.

"Oh, right," Paul said coming to stand by her. "I guess I forgot that I stuck it in my pocket. I meant to tell you."

Margaret looked down at the formal letter in her hand, now wrinkled from its stay in Paul's trousers. "You have been chosen to receive a certificate of honor and the title of Commander of the British Empire for your work in promoting good relationships between India and Great Britain," she read. "Paul, that's wonderful. It means you will receive the gold cross with the picture of King George and Queen Victoria on it. My goodness! I hope you answered this letter!"

"Yes, love, I did. There just isn't any time for me to go to England to get it, but I believe we can pick it all up at the government office in Madras. I suppose I'd better call and arrange to do that." Paul called and the meeting was arranged for the following week.

"And the official I spoke to says we are both invited to lunch," Paul reported.

When the day arrived Margaret came down with a fever. "I just can't go, Paul. You'll have to go alone."

"Since I'm scheduled to make a trip near Madras anyway, I will just stay at a hotel in Madras and go to the government offices the next day before I come home.

I'm sorry you can't make it, Margaret, but it's a long way to go for lunch."

When Paul arrived at the government building in Madras he was surprised to find his daughter, Estelle, and a family friend Margaret had asked to drive her to the luncheon. All three were astounded as they stepped inside onto a red carpet lined with visiting dignitaries, all of whom were there to see Paul honored. The Deputy High Commissioner led the ceremony in place of Her Majesty the Queen. Once again Paul was instructed on what he would be expected to do. As he waited for the ceremony to begin his old friend, Ernest, came to stand close beside him. Paul looked down at his wrinkled suit. He had stayed at a cheap motel last night after traveling all day in the suit he was wearing, the only one he'd brought with him. "Well," he said, "At least I did wear a suit this time." Both men laughed remembering Ernest's efforts to find a suit to fit Paul for the last official reception. Paul hadn't expected any of what he'd found waiting for him at the embassy. He was grateful to his friend, Ernest, and wrinkled or not he was glad he was wearing a suit.

Estelle watched proudly as her father received the highest honor awarded a British subject. She had not dreamed there would be a red carpet, beautifully dressed people, and a grand dinner afterwards, and she would never forget that she had been there to see it all. "You would think, Daddy, your head would get swelled with all the awards and things," she said later. "On the other hand, I guess you're just too busy being a missionary doctor and a builder, and oh, yes," she added teasing him, "a fighter. Mummy always says you go around the world fighting to make the truth known for lepers."

"Well, I won't be going anywhere for awhile until the new rehabilitation and medical building at Vellore is finished." Paul could hardly believe that Vellore would soon have the first building in India for leprosy patients and other disabled patients, a place with plenty of hospital beds, a research room and good equipment, a full rehabilitation program, and even a splint shop to make artificial limbs, braces, surgical shoes, and a host of other needed things. The building was the finest of its kind in orthopedics and leprosy rehabilitation. Many would come from all over the world for training here in India. Surgeons, therapists, and other workers would take what they learned at Vellore to help leprosy patients worldwide. The new building marked the fifteenth year of work at Vellore since its beginnings as a tiny missionary hospital. The President of India, Dr. Sarvapalli himself, came to open the building!

The ancient walls around leprosy were coming down at Vellore. In the new hospital and clinics leprosy would be treated alongside other skin diseases. Paul dreamed of seeing the crumbling of those walls for the millions of lepers around the world.

"It's wonderful," Paul said, picking up a newly-made shoe that John had just completed. "Thanks to you, John, we know how to make the shoes our patients need better than we could have before you came to us. I wish we had more men like you." Paul sat down on an overturned barrel. "We've come a long way with helping our patients, but we've still far to go. John, you and I see how little there is in India for them to do besides beg. The New Life Center with its small crafts to sell just isn't enough. They could work if someone would hire them. I dream of having factories, John, the kind that become part of industry, not sheltered workshops but real factories where our leprosy patients or handicapped persons could work."

John stood to put away his tools. "Paul, you are the only dreamer, builder, surgeon I know, but your dreams have a way of coming true, man. If God puts this in your heart I have no doubt that we'll see those factories right here at Vellore."

Paul and John planned and prayed. Others eager to help joined them, and the first factory in India to employ the disabled opened its doors. Most of the workers were leprosy patients but others were amputees, and those disabled from various causes. They began with making typewriter parts, and soon were doing skilled tool making. It was another dream come true, one that brought the blessing of work to those once barred from the joys that came with a good job.

Vellore and Karigiri were quickly becoming the models for training centers needed all over the world. Paul visited a new site chosen in Addis Ababa, Ethiopia where three thousand lepers lived in the area around a small hospital. He left for home full of enthusiasm, but this time Margaret soon became the center of his attention for the next many weeks.

It was time for a furlough and the family had returned to England when Margaret suddenly felt very sick. Paul was certain that the dengue fever Margaret had suffered in India was the cause of this serious illness. Listless and in extreme pain Margaret needed complete care. Paul became her personal doctor, nurse, cook, housemaid, and more. He did what he could to tempt her appetite with carefully planned meals arranged with flowers on the trays he took to her. The children helped with chores and watched as their doctor father did laundry, cooked, and directed the household. Margaret recovered slowly but at last she was well and Paul decided to take them all on a summer of camping in France and Switzerland. The family was all together and having fun, not yet aware it would be their last time together for a long time. Fall came and with it Paul was called to travel for the mission work on a world tour of duty. He did not see the children again for nearly a year.

Paul's new appointment as full-time director of orthopedics for the Mission to Lepers was not his only work. He was still professor of orthopedic surgery at Vellore, and advisor to the World Health Organization's expert panel on leprosy. Between the three he would spend time in India, England, and wherever in the world his expertise was called for.

One of the highlights of his travels turned out to be in New Guinea. Paul had been asked to go there to advise the government on some plan of action for the many lepers in need of help. The Mission to Lepers wanted to start a work for rehabilitation there, and Paul was to bring back a report on his findings as he traveled the rugged land of Papua New Guinea. Nothing had prepared him for the trip. The small government plane carrying him, Dr. Clezy, a surgeon from Australia, a local government leprosy official, and the pilot, flew over the most wild, rugged, beautiful country he had ever seen. It was the most hair-raising plane ride Paul would ever experience. The small plane struggled to rise up above huge mountain tops, only to dive down the other side whenever they needed to land on one of the tiny airstrips between the tops of the mountain ridges.

Paul quickly realized their pilot had to know the exact lay of the land below them and be an expert in watching out for the updrafts and downdrafts that could catch the little plane and smash it against a mountain. They were in a gorge when the clouds above them began to close in and cover the small opening the pilot was heading for. He turned the plane in a sharp angle and began to retrace his way through the gorge. It was now so narrow Paul worried they would scrape against the tree tops on either side. They made it through but it was not the last time Paul would find himself gripping the seat back in front of him.

They were heading for the final landing strip when the pilot informed his passengers that this landing strip had a continual updraft rushing up the side of the mountain to the edge of the landing site. "If you try to get there straight you can't," he said. "The updraft lifts you so you shoot right past the runway. So, I need to aim for the mountain and just before we might have hit it, that updraft will lift us right onto the runway." Paul hoped and prayed so. But as they headed straight toward the craggy mountain side it was hard not to imagine crashing into it. With bare yards left before they would surely crash, the updraft lifted the plane over the mountain rim and onto the runway. The landing proved smooth, and Paul was grateful and eager to begin the task ahead of them.

"We have many lepers in New Guinea," the government official said, "as you will see, and the need for help is great."

What Paul was about to see in this remote corner of the world would break his heart, and keep him reaching out to do all he could for the lepers God had sent him to love in His name.

Crossroads

"The challenge here is greater than I ever dreamed," Dr. Clezy said. Paul and the doctor had been following their guide to visit remote tribes where many of the people had never been outside their own small territory.

"We've made so much progress in India with our leprosy work that this is like going back to a time before anyone ever heard of rehabilitation for lepers," Paul said. "Don't lose heart," he added, "you're the right man to head the new facility the government wants to set up here. You're a good surgeon and when we get back to Vellore we'll work through techniques and plan together. God has a work here for you to do, and with his help Papua New Guinea will one day be a new Karigiri for these people."

"The sooner the better," the doctor said, stopping to take a rest. "Look over there, Paul," he said pointing to a man not far from them who was walking without any feet at all.

The feet of the lepers here were the worst Paul had seen anywhere. "He is putting all his weight on the ends of his tibial bones," Paul added. It was not the first leper they had seen without feet. Because of the mountainous land with its jagged rocks that tore into a leper's unfeeling flesh and bone there were many such cases. "They cannot help walking their feet off," Paul said. "But even here if these leper patients had been treated early enough and taught to wear shoes they would not be in this sad, terrible condition. And with God's help we'll see that change comes to this place."

By the time they had finished their survey, Paul was able to advise the government where a good leprosy treatment center might do well. Two small Lutheran mission hospitals they had visited could be made into centers for surgery for lepers. Paul would see that the Mission to Lepers sent help through therapists and whatever was available to aid in the new work. On their return to Vellore Dr. Clezy settled into a program of training to prepare him for the work in New Guinea and Paul was soon called to travel again to continue the battle to bring new life to lepers still sitting in darkness and despair in so many places.

Vellore had been the first hospital to open its doors to leper patients, even though they needed to be hidden away in a small, isolated part of the hospital. Paul had seen it grow and helped to build the finest center for leprosy care and rehabilitation in India at Vellore. A few miles away Paul had helped plan and watch Karigiri, the first leprosy hospital and rehabilitation center just for lepers, become a beautiful oasis in the desert. "It amazes me," he told

Margaret one day, "how far the word has spread about Vellore and Karigiri." Now he was invited to lecture and share his expertise on leprosy in places as far away as Ethiopia, the Philippines, Hong Kong, South Africa, South East Asia, Australia, Canada, Thailand, as well as in his homeland England.

More and more on his travels he was finding former students back in their own countries who now struggled to teach the new ways of treating lepers they had learned in Vellore and Karigiri. "Thanks to visits with your old students, you at least get a day off now and then," Margaret noted. Much of the time on his travels Paul's schedule left no room at all for a day off. He had gone as long as two full months with only one day in each month not heavily scheduled.

Paul had sometimes arrived by plane in the morning, spoken to newspaper journalists at the airport, and gone on to do interviews the very same day at radio or TV stations. After lunch at a hospital he would lecture to the medical students or a group of doctors. Afternoons were often at women's meetings with tea, and evenings at church services. The following day he visited the hospital, and sometimes operated, might have lunch with an interested club group, and another church meeting in the evening. This pattern of two-day stays with a travel day between them went on and on. Paul had once counted seventy-four trips by plane. To Margaret, Paul confessed that he often felt like a kind of celebrity and it embarrassed him.

All except once, at a radio interview which still made him chuckle.

The talk show host didn't seem to know much about Paul and his work or leprosy, and Paul had the feeling the man was a little bored with the subject. His host began by saying, "I suppose you treat lepers. Why is it they need someone like you to help them?"

Paul replied with a few sentences about leprosy and the problems it causes, and added casually, "And some of them don't even have cats."

His host seemed to think Paul was making a joke. "All right," he said, "What is so bad about their not having a cat?"

Paul went on to tell about leprosy patients' lack of feeling pain in their hands or feet. "So in Indian villages the rats soon learn how safely and easily they can take a bite, even a whole finger or toe, from an unfeeling hand or foot of a sleeping man. A cat next to the bed takes the place of the warning pain would give," Paul said. The interview planned for 5-10 minutes went on for thirty.

"How can you pack so much into your days, sometimes twelve hours of operating, teaching, research, writing, and all the rest of your responsibilities?" someone at Vellore had once asked Paul.

"I never could, if I didn't take time every morning without exception to place the day before the Lord," Paul said. Those meetings between Heaven and

Earth before his work day began were a lifelong commitment for him. Many years later Paul insisted it was what made it possible to accomplish the tasks before him.

Back home Paul was beginning to think about the future. He could keep dividing his time between Vellore, England with the family, and missions to other countries, or go fully into research, look for new techniques in surgery, share more and write more of God's wonderful works in his creation, his love!

"It would be wonderful to be in England with our growing family" Margaret said one evening as they sat on the verandah sipping cool tea. "We have such fine help here now that I don't think I'd be much missed. Not that I'd want to stop working in eye treatment," she said.

"I think you have been reading my mind lately," Paul teased. "I've asked myself if I could be more useful somewhere besides here in India. You're right, we couldn't ask for better surgeons and staff than we have here and at Karigiri. I know your patients would miss you, my dear, but I've already been traveling so much I doubt I'd be missed."

"Well, your family has missed you a great deal, and I for one would love to see more of you," Margaret teased.

"Now that we know Mother won't leave the Kollis, and is really loving what she does there, I don't worry about her," Paul mused.

"She has to be the only eighty-four-year-old woman who is still traveling the mountains to as many villages as she can reach with the gospel, to say nothing of the schools she still oversees and all those unwanted children she sees to," Margaret said. "Every time we've visited her in the Kollis, I see the love of the people for her. Everyone in the hills knows who she is, the old woman who loves them and preaches the love of Jesus."

"She is a marvel to me," Paul agreed. "She'll be a missionary to the end of her life on earth. I promised we would honor her wish to be buried on the Kollis next to my father when the time comes."

"She is proud of you, Paul, and of Connie too," Margaret said.

"The last time I saw Connie she was far too skinny, but utterly happy. She does love her work in Africa with her husband. She's teaching children, training teachers, and even writing books for the children. She's not in India like we both thought we'd be when we were little, but she is every bit the missionary we wanted to be."

Margaret was back in England with the children when Paul received a call from the United States Public Health facility for lepers at Carville, Louisiana. The new director at Carville wanted Paul to come and establish a program of rehabilitation for their lepers. It was the only federally-funded leprosy center in the United States. "We have enough money to allow you all the travel you might need to do, and whatever you will need for the program here," the director said. "We'll also open an ophthalmology position for Margaret to continue her work with leprosy patients here."

Paul was excited. This might be God's next path for him. He promised to talk to Margaret and the children. It meant another move for the family after twenty years in India. This time it would not be a return to their homeland England, but to a new culture in the United States. Life in the American culture would be quite different for them all, and especially for the children who would have to change schools. He made the phone call to Margaret and asked her to discuss the move with the children and have the family all vote on it.

Margaret and the children studied maps, read about Louisiana and Carville and took the vote. It was unanimous. Even Jean voted yes, though she would stay in England to finish nursing school. The move was arranged, and whatever lay ahead at Carville, Paul felt eager for the challenge.

Carville

Paul and the family came to Carville during the winter of 1966. The setting with its large oak trees, hanging Spanish moss, 400 acres of fields, a lake, horses and cattle grazing was inviting. But quickly the children spotted the high fence running between the road and the grounds. "Why is there a fence everywhere?" young Estelle asked.

"The fence is to keep out tourists or anyone who doesn't belong inside the hospital grounds," Paul explained. "The hospital has some rules that we'll all have to get used to, I'm afraid." He knew the children hadn't seen the kind of segregation in India that they would find at Carville. "Not so many years ago these grounds would have been filled with yellow quarantine flags to warn people not to come near the hospital or patients' quarters. Barbed wire fencing used to be here before the present fence. Things are better now, but you will not be allowed in patients' housing, nor will they be allowed to visit staff housing. No one under age sixteen can go near patient areas. These are the rules, and we expect you children to follow them."

"But, Daddy, everyone knows that leprosy is only contagious for a little while until the germs that cause it are killed. And anyway, you told us most adult people are immune to leprosy." Mary said. She considered herself close enough to adulthood to qualify as one. "Look out the window at those older patients who are walking around near the hospital. I just know they'd probably love to visit with us," she added.

"True," Paul said, "and you all do know the basic truths about the disease of leprosy, but that doesn't change the rules here. Good things have started happening here and that is certainly part of the work we've been asked to do. In time the hope is to make Carville as fine for its lepers as Karigiri and Vellore is for ours." Paul still spoke of his beloved Indian leprosy patients as if he were just away from them for a time. His love and care for lepers had begun at Chingleput, India on the day he saw his first leper's clawed hands. All those years in India Paul had loved his patients with Jesus' love as he worked to restore their damaged bodies.

"Daddy," Pauline asked, "Tell us a story about the old times here, please." Paul was a true storyteller and his storytelling never disappointed his children. Pauline really wanted to hear about the bad things the poor lepers had put up with in Carville's early days.

"Well, for one thing all the patients' mail had to go through a sterilization process before they could mail it. That was a government law. The doctors and staff at Carville knew that putting all the mail into an oven to sterilize it wasn't needed and really a waste of time, but the government law said it must be done." Paul saw their new house up ahead and slowed the car. "We'll have to save the rest until another time; we're here!" The house was on the hospital grounds and close to the Mississippi River levee, a perfect place for a family of active, free-spirited children to roam.

The family did love their home, and settled in quickly. The real work of adjusting came when the girls began attending school. Southern schools were full of the Civil Rights movement at this time. The girls saw first hand what segregation in the South meant.

Paul fit into his new work easily, bringing to it the same love and care for each patient as he had in India. The older patients were soon sharing their stories of the old days with him. "Those were the days when lepers had no rights, no vote, and no voice about their lives," one said. "Even in the 1950s, some patients were brought here in chains. You couldn't leave here back then, though some patients slipped under the fence and escaped. But if you did the sheriff would go after you, and you could land in prison. Lepers were quarantined by law everywhere in the country, and lepers can't hide easily," he added.

"And another thing about the sheriff," one of the patients said, "before I came here I had a wife and children. But back then even if your family wanted you, it meant hiding out, or else they'd come and take you away from your family, like the sheriff did with me. It was all legal too. Once folks knew you were a leper you weren't wanted, and the law said you needed to be put in quarantine." The old man shook his head remembering the past. "This place was like a prison then," he said.

"Yes, sir," another said, "tore families apart more than once in those times. If you look out at the cemetery here you can find names on the stones that lepers used to take to protect their families from trouble. A leper in a family made the whole family suspect.

Sometimes a leper would come and say his name and it would turn out he'd picked it off a store brand. You still see 'em on the tombstones."

Paul learned that Carville had started in secrecy as a haven for lepers nobody wanted. The old deserted plantation house with its run-down former slave cabins had been purchased under the disguise of being bought for an ostrich farm. Back then no leper could take any kind of public transportation, so the first lepers were brought in secretly by river barge. The only ones who would come and care for them were nuns. Paul had seen some of the hard work, the gardens and the building the nuns had worked on still stood on the grounds. Thankfully, things were changing here, and Paul discovered one day that his youngest daughter, Pauline had her own plan to help.

Paul had come home for a late afternoon tea. Sipping his tea as he looked out the front window at

Pauline, who was standing by the fence near the road, he saw the most unusual sight.

Just as a car came up the road it slowed and its passengers leaned out the windows to have a look at the grounds. Tourists often did so hoping to see lepers, Paul knew. Suddenly Pauline looked as if she were going into some sort of dance. She balled up her hands and waved them frantically. Now and then she leaned sideways and limped. When Paul got a look at her face it was screwed up in the worst grimace he'd seen her make, and she knew how to make them! He shook his head, and then began laughing. His daughter was doing her best to frighten away the tourists by pretending to be a leper, and what looked like a fierce one.

When Paul asked for an explanation, she said. "Daddy, the tourists come and they stare like this was a zoo for lepers. It's just not right! I don't mind scaring them away one bit."

"I'm sure you don't," Paul said. "But maybe what tourists really need is to learn about leprosy, things you already know, Pauline. Tourist tours can be a good thing, once people know the truth about leprosy they can spread the word to others." Pauline nodded; at least, Paul thought, she might think better about her actions. In time tourist tours were scheduled, and did enlighten some folks, though the stigma attached to leprosy, called Hansen's disease at Carville, would remain for many.

Paul and Margaret were fully involved in the work at Carville, each with their own specialty. They were finding that here too the same longing to appear normal was as strong as it was back in India. As soon as a patient was declared no longer positive for leprosy bacilli they could try to find work off the grounds, visit the town café and go about freely. Margaret had one woman patient whose social life was putting her eyes in great danger. The young woman painted eyebrows and lashes on with heavy black mascara. The eyes were already showing signs of damage from the mascara so frequently poked into them.

"Look," she said to Susie, her patient. "Even when I've watched you stand before a mirror to put on your make-up, I've seen your fingers slip and the mascara poke into your eye. Your fingers just can't feel anything, I know, but if this keeps on you could lose your sight."

"Oh, but I need to wear make-up just to look like everybody else, you know," the young woman replied. "And I will be careful," she promised.

Margaret tried to explain that no amount of promising to be careful, even though she meant it, would keep those unfeeling fingers from poking mascara into her eyes.

"Well, I'm working now and I really do need this make-up. Honestly, I will be really careful and you'll see," the woman said. Margaret felt only sadness because in time this young woman might not see at all.

Paul's thoughts these days centered once again on shoes. All the work at Vellore and Karigiri had proven that lepers needed to wear shoes. In India Paul and the team had to educate their patients, especially those in the villages, not to go barefoot. Here at Carville his patients wore shoes, just not the right kind. Most wore the fashionable shoes others were wearing, often narrow and pointed ones. Feet that felt no pain could be squeezed into fashionable shoes, but at a terrible price. At the foot clinic they treated those same feet for the same ugly ulcers they'd seen in India. The clinic did provide orthopedic shoes that properly fitted to a patient's foot would help prevent damage, but some patients refused to wear the thick, heavy-looking orthopedic shoes.

One of Paul's young patients, Jimmy, liked to dress fashionably for his job, and chose to wear narrow pointed shoes because they were in style. He had already refused to wear orthopedic shoes in spite of Paul's gentle warnings. "If you insist on fashion, than at least buy shoes a size larger for the sake of your feet and let me line them with a soft lining," Paul urged him. Again and again as Jimmy repeatedly came back to the clinic for foot treatments, and Paul patiently cared for him, he would try to persuade him to do something about his tight shoes.

"Well, maybe, but I don't feel any pain, you know" Jimmy would assure him. Paul's deep concern for Jimmy and his gentle care continued, but he never was able to convince Jimmy to change his mind. In time the young man lost all of his toes and only mere stumps of feet remained, still hidden in narrow fashionable shoes. Paul made a hospital rule that patients must at least change their shoes every five hours.

Thankfully, the research Paul and his staff were doing showed great results. This was the breakthrough they needed to prevent foot damage before it started. With the arrival of a new thermograph machine Paul had ordered they could now see beneath the skin's surface any warm spots not yet noticeable above the skin. Up until this time Paul's sensitive hands could feel a hot spot on the surface skin of a patient's foot and know that an ulcer was coming. But before the thermograph machine no one had known that a warm area below the skin's surface could signal danger even before it reached the skin. Immediate rest of the foot soon relieved the hidden irritation keeping it from erupting and damaging tissue. The machine became a routine part of a patient's checkup at the foot clinic. Paul was delighted! Prevention was the best of cures.

Even Margaret and the children were amazed at Paul's next experiment. This time Paul was hoping to at last shed light on one of the mysteries about lepers' feet still unsolved. His years of searching for a good shoe back at Vellore had taught him how dangerous small repeated pressures were to a leper's foot. But no one had figured out why simply walking long distances was dangerous for a leper's feet, but not for a normal person's. For Paul's new research, all over Carville's grounds a small army of volunteers, both staff and patients, walked carefully measured amounts wearing Paul's newly invented slipper sox inside their shoes.

The slipper sox of soft foam were filled with tiny wax microcapsules of dye. Under the pressure of walking the wax would melt and mark the pressure points in blue dye. For Paul to see what difference the length of a walk made, his volunteers went on walks some longer, some shorter. With the help of a volunteer staff who enjoyed running Paul mapped the pressures on feet from running. They soon learned what happened with each measured lap. After thousands of mappings with the help of his willing staff and patients the mystery was solved!

Paul now knew that lepers never change their stride. The blue dye mappings showed the clear difference between their walking and a normal person's. "See here," Paul explained pointing to the charts before him, "how a normal person changes his stride as he walks, and the longer the person walks the more he changes his stride. With each change of stride the pressures on the feet changed too." He turned to face the group of doctors and therapists listening. "The whole process of changing strides is done subconsciously, as you know. As the skin of the feet feel too much pressure in one place they send a signal to the spinal cord and lower brain to change the stride and spread out the pressure." Paul paused before he said, "Since the skin on a leper's feet feels nothing it sends no signals. Lepers never change their stride, and the pressures on a leper's feet are not relieved." Around the room Paul heard murmurs of assent. "It's like someone clapping their hands together hour after hour," he said, "pressures on the leper's feet are not relieved and that, gentlemen, leads to damage." The group of doctors and therapists in front of him already knew that the leprosy patients would never feel the damage, even when tissues broke down and deep ulcers formed, exposing bone. A leper would not even limp. For the rest of his life a leper whose disease had been healed would face the terrible problems of living with unfeeling hands and feet. Leprosy patients needed shoes to help spread the pressures of walking, and they needed to know that they must not walk long distances ever. Shutting his lecture book, Paul said, "Gentlemen and ladies, once the battle was to let the world know that leprosy doesn't make the flesh rot. Our next step was to open what had been a closed door to reconstructing damaged limbs. What we know now for certain about the pressures on our leprosy patients' feet, truly is a great step forward that will help us with preventing damage before it begins. That is a far better help to our patients."

As they were leaving the room Paul overheard a whispered comment from an elderly visitor, one that made him shake his head.

"Yes, yes, but so much research on lepers to find out they must not walk too much, I can't see how it's worth time and money spent on such projects." Worth it? Paul thought. His mind went back to the very first operation he had done to straighten a leper's badly twisted feet. He saw again the face of Krishnamurthy when he had first come to Vellore, his eyes full of misery and pain caused by a life of cruel treatment and rejection from the world around him. And then Krishnamurthy with new hands and feet, a smile, Christ in his heart, and a new life ahead of him. Paul had known it was all worth it then. He would have liked to take that man to meet some of his patients.

Lou was one of those patients. As Paul stepped into Lou's room the old man, a native of Hawaii, whose leprosy had left him deaf, unable to feel, and nearly blind, was singing. Paul stood in the doorway listening to the hymn Lou sang as he strummed the auto harp on his lap with the special glove the therapists had made to keep his hand from damage. After awhile Paul left without disturbing him.

Over the years Paul's work as Director of Rehabilitation at Carville accomplished more than he'd first dreamed. It was all part of serving the Lord as a missionary doctor. Carville was supported by government funds and had become the modern, fine rehabilitation and research center for leprosy Paul had hoped for. The beautiful grounds and buildings were no longer fenced. Patients were free to roam, and all kinds of equipment and events were available to them. Paul loved his patients, especially those few cases like Lou, elderly patients whose disease had left them almost shut off from the world. Lou was a member of the small Carville church Paul and Margaret attended. Each Sunday Lou played his auto harp and sang for them. Lou, the harpist loved the Lord and though he could feel nothing and see nothing and his hearing too was fading, his songs to the Lord were a gift. No songs were sweeter to Paul and Margaret's ears than this dear leper's. Paul could do nothing more for Lou but Lou continued to give his gift of music to them. Was this dear leper worth all the love and care they could give him in Jesus' name? Paul's heart overflowed with a mighty "Yes!"

Meanwhile, during their twenty years at Carville the children had grown and left the nest. Mary had wanted her wedding in Carville's plantation house, but felt sad that no patients would be allowed to attend. Estelle had grown into a lovely young woman and married a former leprosy patient. They were living in Hawaii. Paul knew that the work at Carville no longer really needed him, and he had also begun to feel a gentle inner prodding that made him think it might be time to move on.

Paul's hair was no longer brown and there was less of it, his face a bit more wrinkled, and he was in his seventies. "Margaret, I've been thinking," he began one evening, "maybe the Lord is prompting me to make a change."

Before he could say another word, Margaret looked up from the papers on her lap. "I think I know what you are about to say: retirement," she said. "Isn't it wonderful that God so many times brings each of us to think the same thoughts about his next step for us? I've been having those same gentle promptings you've had so many times when we were to make a move, or a big decision."

Paul sat beside her, a cup of tea in his hand. "The Leprosy Mission wants me to continue acting as Medical Consultant to the mission, and the World Health Organization is asking me to continue in my advisory role, so we won't exactly be without something to do," he said.

"True," Margaret added, "and there is all the writing you are doing too. I, of course, plan to be a busy grandmother as well." The phone rang and Margaret went to another room to answer. She was expecting a call from Mary.

Paul smiled broadly already thinking how blessed they were and what joys lay ahead. The years in Carville had been good ones. Looking back Paul thought of their days in India. How many thousands of times had he looked at a patient's face and hands and feet and seen beyond broken limbs to someone precious to God who longed to heal their broken hearts and lives. It had guided his hands in every operation, and his heart in love for them all. Paul's slipperless feet rested on a foot stool in front of him. He wiggled his toes and wiggled them again, feeling the movement of them, the privilege of feeling them.

How many hundreds of shoes he and his team had fashioned to find the one that would save a leper's unfeeling feet from the pressures that would wound his flesh and bone. How many years of research, of fighting to prove that those feet could be protected, the terrible damage even prevented! Paul's eyes filled as he remembered the battle to show the world the truth about leprosy, and the stigma that still lingered in places. Paul looked at his hands remembering how it felt to fashion a shoe, to fit the soft inner lining to a foot. How privileged these hands had been to build, to operate, to comfort those Jesus had loved and touched, lepers precious to him.

Paul looked again at his own bare feet that had never worn shoes when he'd been a boy running and climbing the Kolli Hills. Those feet had carried him a long way since then on paths he could never have dreamed to take. Sometimes he'd thought God had made a mistake. Who would have imagined that the schoolboy who disappointed everyone with his grades, would become a surgeon and love research? Paul chuckled remembering how sure he'd been that he'd missed God's plan and wasted years training to be a builder! The war years, all the times he had thought unplanned, had been part of God's plan all along. What shoes visible only to God had covered his child's bare feet, protected them and guided them all these years? Were they the unseen shoes God's love fashioned for each of his children, shoes made from his love? Paul wiggled his splendid, God-created toes, and smiled. When a leprosy patient put on the special shoes made for him Paul knew how many hours of loving research, hours of loving labor were behind that shoe and the shoes before that one. His eyes again filled with tears. A greater love had made the shoes that guided his feet all his life on each path, in each battle, to each joy. The more he walked in them, the more he knew it was so. Connie's feet now in Africa serving the Lord, his mother's old feet still serving him in the Kollis, Margaret's and the children's serving him, all of them wore the shoes God's love made. Paul smiled thinking he and his team would have given every leper on earth shoes to protect their feet if they could have. God did better. His love fashioned shoes for every one of his children, shoes that never wore out, shoes that cared for their feet all along the path.

"We may be entering retirement," Paul said as Margaret returned. "But our shoes aren't worn out yet, and they won't be until the last step this side of heaven." Margaret looked a bit puzzled and Paul smiled broadly.

A Word from the Author

A Word from the Author

The years ahead would bring Paul and Margaret to Seattle, where Paul became Clinical Professor of Orthopedics, Emeritus at the University of Washington. He would also be President of the Leprosy Mission International from 1993-1999. His book on hand surgery, The Clinical Mechanics of the Hand, is still used in medical schools today. Retirement made it possible for Paul to write more about the wonders of God's love, the marvels of the human body and its lessons until his final meeting with Heaven in 2003.

Just the other day, I met a missionary who had known Paul Brand when Paul was in Ethiopia helping to plan a new work for lepers there. Not long before that I met an Indian woman working in the local bank whose in-laws back in India work at Vellore, the very hospital where Paul operated on his first leprosy patient, the first operation ever done to reconstruct a leper's hand. The story goes on all over the world today and the shoes love made reach everywhere.

Paul Brand Time Line

1914   Paul Wilson Brand born in India.

1918   Armistice ends World War I.

1922   First portable radio and car radio made in the United States.

1923   Paul sent to the United Kingdom for education.

1926   John Logie Baird invented the television.

1928   Paul's father dies.

1930   White women given the vote in South Africa.

1939   Germany invades Poland, leading to World War II.

1940   British scientists develop radar.

1945   US scientists build first atomic bomb.

1946   Paul invited to join staff of the Christian Medical College and Hospital in Vellore, India. He went on to develop treatments for leprosy sufferers and people with diabetes.

1948   Israeli independence leads to the first Arab-Israeli war.

1952   Paul awarded the Hunterian Professorship of the Royal College of Surgeons.

1953   DNA discovered.

1953   Paul and his wife, Margaret, join the staff of the Leprosy Mission.

1960   Paul awarded the Albert Laskar Award.

1961   Paul honoured by Queen Elizabeth with a title of the Commander of the Order of the British Empire.

1964   Paul appointed the Leprosy Mission's Director of Surgery and Rehabilitation.

1966	Paul moved to the U.S.A. to work as Chief of the Rehabilitation Branch at the National Hansen's Disease Centre at Carville.
1969	US astronauts Neil Armstrong and Edwin Aldrin land on the moon.
1974	US president Nixon resigns after Watergate scandal.
1977	Paul receives the Damian-Dutton Award.
1979	Britain elects first female prime minister, Margaret Thatcher.
1980	Iran-Iraq war breaks out.
1982	Falklands War between Argentina and Britain.
1986	Paul retires from the U.S. Public Health Service, moves to Seattle and continues teaching as emeritus professor of Orthopedics in the University of Washington.
1989	Berlin Wall dismantled.
2003	Paul dies from complications related to a subdural hematoma.

BIBLIOGRAPHY

BOOKS

Brand, Paul, *Clinical Mechanics of the Hand*, Mosby, St. Louis MO, 1999.

Brand, Paul and Philip Yancey, *Fearfully and Wonderfully Made*, Zondervan, Grand Rapids MI, 1980.

Brand, Paul and Philip Yancey, *The Gift of Pain: Why We Hurt and What We Can Do About It,* Zondervan, Grand Rapids MI, 1997.

Brand, Paul and Philip Yancey, *In His Image*, Zondervan, Grand Rapids MI, 1984.

Brand, Paul and Philip Yancey, *Pain: The Gift Nobody Wants*, Harper Collins Publishers, New York, 1993.

Wilson, Dorothy Clarke, *Ten Fingers for God*, McGraw-Hill Book Company, New York, 1965.

Wilson, Dorothy Clarke, *Granny Brand: Her Story*, Paul Brand Publishing, Seattle WA, 1976.

ARTICLES

Brand, Paul, "Blood: The Miracle of Life," *Christianity Today* 27: March 4, 1983: 38-42.

Brand, Paul, "Life in the Blood," *Christianity Today* 27: March 18, 1983: 18-21.

Brand, Paul, "Blood: The Miracle of Cleansing," *Christianity Today* 27: April 5, 1983: 12-15.

Brand, Paul, "A Surgeon's View of Divine Healing," *Christianity Today* 27: November 25, 1983: 14-21.

Brand, Paul, "The Scars of Easter," *Christianity Today* 29: April 5, 1985: 20-21.

Note: Dorothy Clarke's *Ten Fingers for God*, her excellent biography of Dr. Brand's life, was immensely helpful to me in bringing together the many events of Paul Brand's life found in his own writings and others as I worked on this Trailblazer book, *The Shoes that Love Made.*

Thinking Further

1. The Mountains of Death
As the son of missionaries in India, Paul lived on the Kollis Mountains along with wild animals, scorpions, snakes, and diseases. His parents trusted God and taught Paul to do the same. You may live in a very different kind of place and face different dangers and challenges. Discuss God's power to keep us no matter where we live. What does the Bible tell us about his power, his rule over the earth and people? See Romans 8: 38,39 and Matthew 28:18.

2. In England You Wear Shoes
What brought the pujari (village priest) to see the difference between his demon gods and Jesus? How can we show the love of Jesus to others?

When Paul and his family went on furlough back to England it meant moving to a strange place for Paul. Something as small as having to wear shoes became a problem to him. Discuss how either you or others you know may find having to move to a different place difficult. Do you know any immigrant students who may be trying to adjust to a new culture? How can it help us to know that others may be finding it hard to learn new ways? How can we show Jesus' love to them?

3. Left Behind

When Paul was a boy attending school in England he was separated from his parents who were back in India for many years at a time. What Scripture on his bedroom wall comforted him? Think of the promises of Jesus to help us when we are lonely or sad. Does God keep his promises? Can we take Jesus at his word?

4. A Cancelled Furlough

Paul felt like a misfit in the family when he saw all the things the rest of the family did well and couldn't think of anything he did well. Sometimes we may feel that way too. What kind of brother was Paul to Connie? What things did he do well? What does God's word say about encouraging others? How was Paul's love of nature, climbing trees and enjoying summer with his cousins good for him? Why do you think enjoying God's creation is a good thing? Remember the verses on Paul's bedroom wall; do our failures keep us from our mother's love or God's?

5. A Father's Final Letter

News of the death of Paul's father came so unexpectedly to Paul and Connie that they were grieved and shocked for many weeks. Discuss how sudden loss through death can happen to Christian families today. How did his father's death affect Paul's mother? Neither Paul nor his mother lost their trust in God but it took time and loving family to help them over their grief. Discuss how grief affects us. How does belonging to Jesus make a difference? When God sent Mr. Warwick the builder into Paul's life he was greatly comforted by the unexpected chance to become a builder. Can we expect God's working in our lives even after great loss like the death of a parent? Read Jeremiah 29:11.

6. Life in Two Worlds

How did Paul's attitude about studying change once he became an apprentice in the building trade? When we "feel" right about the things we are doing how does that affect our efforts?

Paul wanted to share the life of his fellow laborers and he learned to speak their language and wear the same clothes. When he became a doctor to lepers he learned to speak their language and feel their troubles, often spending hours watching them work at Vellore to understand their needs. Discuss how we can learn to reach out to others who are different from us? What examples does Jesus give us in Scripture?

7. A World Upside Down

When Paul was a young boy why didn't he think he would ever be a doctor? What made Paul change his mind about becoming a doctor? Do the fears and dislikes we have as we are growing up determine how we can serve God in the future?

When Paul was in medical school he thought he had wasted four years of his life learning the building trade.

When he and Margaret were ready to go to the mission field it looked like World War II and the army would send him to the Far East instead. Paul believed God was still watching over them and always guiding them, and God did make it possible for Paul to be released from the army and go to India as a missionary doctor. Discuss the times in our lives when we may wonder if we are on the right track. What does the Bible tell us about God's guidance for us? See John 14:15 and John 16:13.

8. Chingleput

When Paul Brand first began working with lepers how did most of the world act towards them? How did Paul and Margaret see their leprosy patients? How did Jesus feel about lepers? Does the world see people the way God does? Are there students at your school or others you know who are not treated well because they are different? How should Christians treat others?

How did God use Paul's building skills even though he was trained as a surgeon? Does this make you think God can use your skills and the things you enjoy doing even if he leads you down a different path in the future? Do you think God has plans for each of us?

9. Cuts and Blisters, Rats and Cats

A leper's hands and feet that never feel pain don't even feel a nail in their foot or a hot metal pot in their hand. How can pain be a blessing? The Bible says that by Jesus' wounds we are healed, and for the joy set before him he endured the shame (the painful shame) of the cross. What blessing comes to us through Jesus' pain? When we are suffering pain what has Jesus said that can help us?

10. I Was a Stranger

Why did Paul's wife, Margaret, invite a leper to stay with them until Paul returned to see him? What did Jesus say about the way we treat strangers or needy people? Though Paul was becoming famous for his work and received a Rockefeller grant to travel worldwide to research and teach about leprosy, as well as the highest honor given in Surgery in Great Britain, he discovered after all his travels that only one doctor was doing hand surgery on lepers' hands. What was the belief about leprosy that Paul was battling? Why was this such an important battle?

11. Cut Them Off Sahib

Paul's work to restore the feet and hands of leprosy patients gave them back the ability to be useful. But leprosy often disfigured its victims and even after they were no longer contagious people shunned them. Helping to remove the signs of leprosy from their faces made it possible for cured lepers to be able to go back to their villages and families. Discuss how our world often looks at disabled people today, especially those who have deformities. Is it important for Christians to do all we can to love and accept and help others the world rejects because they are not beautiful or whole? What does the Bible say?

Joni Eareckson Tada's organization gives wheelchairs to disabled people all over the world. Discuss how this important work helps in the teaching of the gospel.

12. See for Yourself, Sir

Many visitors to the Vellore conference on leprosy were convinced by what they saw that they had been wrong about leprosy making bad flesh. How did the movie Paul's friend made help the Ministry to Lepers? Discuss the many ways of teaching the gospel we have today. Can God use some of us to become skilled in technology to serve him? Discuss the gifts of the Holy Spirit in Ephesians 4. Pray for God to guide each of us to the profession and skills he wants us to use for his kingdom work.

13. Her Majesty the Queen

Paul Brand received many honors for his work, but he was often surprised by them. His heart and mind were truly full of the love of God and the work he was called to do, and. he often felt overflowing thankfulness to God. If honors come our way how should we treat them as God's children? Does God reward his children? Discuss what Jesus says about this in Scriptures. Read Matthew 5: 1-12.

14. The 5 p.m. Committee

Why do you think the 5 p.m. committee meeting was so important to Paul that he wrote it on his calendar? Is spending time with our families important enough for us to set time aside for family even when we are busy? Discuss how Jesus' command to love one another includes family. What ways might we think of to do this?

15. Crossroads

Discuss the terrible conditions of the lepers in New Guinea when Paul and his friend first went there to plan a new work among them. Our world has so many places even today where people suffer from poverty and oppression and need the good news of Jesus. Discuss how God is using his people to serve today in some of these places. How can we help?

16. Carville

At Carville Paul at last discovered the difference between a leper's walk and a normal person's walk. Why was this such a great discovery? He and Margaret also learned that some leprosy patients refused to do what would keep them from severe damage from leprosy. How did Paul act towards such a patient? At the end of this chapter Paul thinks about the years of loving labor and research he and his team did to find the right shoes for a leper's feet. He also thinks back on his own childhood days and running barefoot on the Kollis. As he remembers how God has guided his feet throughout his life he thinks of the spiritual kind of shoes God who loves his children makes for their feet. Read Ephesians 6. We cannot see the shoes God has made for us but we know they are part of his clothing for us. Discuss how our feet are protected and guided along God's path for us.

CHRISTIAN FOCUS PUBLICATIONS

Christian Focus | Christian Heritage | CF4K | Mentor

Christian Focus Publications publishes books for adults and children under its four main imprints: Christian Focus, CF4K, Mentor and Christian Heritage. Our books reflect that God's Word is reliable and Jesus is the way to know him, and live for ever with him.

Our children's publication list includes a Sunday School curriculum that covers pre-school to early teens; puzzle and activity books. We also publish personal and family devotional titles, biographies and inspirational stories that children will love.

If you are looking for quality Bible teaching for children then we have an excellent range of Bible story and age specific theological books.

From pre-school to teenage fiction, we have it covered!

Find us at our web page:
www.christianfocus.com

CF4•K
Because you're never
too young to know Jesus